Musings of a Housework Avoidance Expert

50 Tiny Tales

By Charmaine Welch

Filidh Publishing

For Jenny, my favourite daughter, Mike, my favourite oldest son, Max, my favourite middle son, and Rudy, my favourite youngest son. Love you forever and always — and then some! I couldn't have done life without you.

Contents

Preface

This eclectic collection of 50 tiny tales is my written account of thoughts on incidents I have encountered during my ordinary life.

With my age count rising (68 at present) my mind drifts, unbidden, to my eventual demise. While pondering what to leave my descendants as my legacy, I decided words in the form of this book are probably the most enduring way vestiges of my essence might live on.

What the heck is this book about, anyway? Is it a manual on how not to clean your house? What does it signify?

Calm yourself, dear reader. I will explain. I am a fervent and hyper-focused Maker. Making "stuff" has always brought me great satisfaction. Sometimes it's of practical use, sometimes not. Sewing is my favourite medium, but I have been known to try many other creative pursuits.

I do not subscribe to the Martha Stewart method of devoting my entire existence to the decoration and upkeep of our house and home. Slap happy is much closer to my style of domestic science. My husband heartily concurs that this is the case.

The "Musings" component of my title is a nod to my humble stint as an occasional columnist for our local monthly newspaper called Metchosin Muse. I am forever in Jo Mitchell's debt for setting me on the path towards this book.

The "expert" moniker I bestowed on myself is the response I give to people's comments on my prolific accumulation of products I vend. My standard response is "This is a result of my housework avoidance program".

People seem to understand my viewpoint of choosing to make stuff over cleaning. If I am productive, I can be forgiven the faint sheen of dust on the furniture. OK, OK. There's more than a sheen. That's why our lights are dimmed so low.

A short explanation of the front and rear cover photographs is in order. The front cover shows me at approximately the age I was when I began writing the stories in this book. The back cover shows me as I am today. I like the symbolism.

My thought is that this compilation would be a great book to pick up and read when you need a short break. The stories are quite benign and, I hope, amusing. Being that the stories are short, knocking off several tiny true tales may be just the pick-me-up you need. Not instead of coffee, of course, but in addition to your java, (or tea or kombucha, or filtered water etc.)

I hope you, gentle reader, enjoy my jottings.

Duped

When we speak of New Year's resolutions, the one frequently mentioned is the desire to lose weight. On the subject of weight loss, let me tell you a tale from my long ago past.

I wasn't a fat kid. Not a chubby teenager, either.

My extra weight accumulated after I left home and moved to Port McNeill to work. I boarded with a family who served cream sauces on all their vegetables and half the meat. I had come from a plain meat-and-vegetable family and thought all these fancy meals heavenly.

Port McNeill in the early 70s didn't offer a lot of leisure activities, so I kept busy hosting fondue parties. Oil fondue in one pot, cheese fondue in the second pot, and, yes, chocolate fondue in the third, for dessert. I wasn't fond of most alcoholic drinks but found one that I enjoyed very much — you guessed it! Kahlua and cream.

Are you getting an expanded picture of me? In one year, I gained 20 pounds. TWENTY POUNDS!

My problem was that I had fat-gram ignorance. I had no knowledge of what fat grams were or where they lived.

Fortrel pants and hunched shoulders helped me cope for a few years until I joined Weight Watchers. Their program really helped me take control of my eating habits and gave me a good nutritional grounding. I lost my excess 20 pounds, then went on to become a vegetarian. By then I was really aware of where the fat hides out and I lost an additional 15 pounds.

At 105 pounds, I was quite slim, but still not pleased with my "look". All my life I had been told by magazines and television that all I needed to be happy was to lose my extra weight. I had worked hard, forsaken chocolate, and had attained a slender physique. Why was satisfaction eluding me? I was about to find out.

I was looking through pattern books at the fabric store one day, admiring the slim silhouettes of the models in the photos, when the reality of my situation hit me.

Wait for it! Here it comes! I wasn't

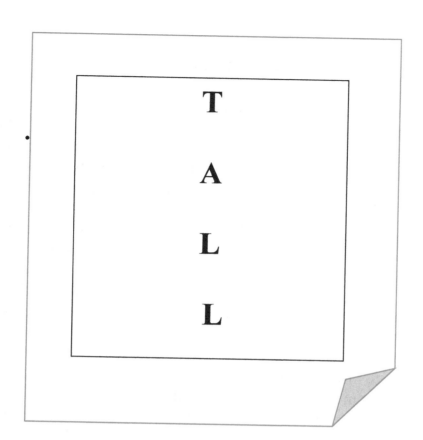

Musings on Housekeeping

I bet you are wondering about my housekeeping methods. My standard flippant answer is that I don't do housework. Of course I do housework, I just don't take it as seriously as some of my friends. I maintain a standard that would probably pass a Social Services inspection (How strict ARE they, do you suppose?)

My basic philosophy of cleaning is to clean as I notice it's dirty. This presents several problems. Generally, I'm not very observant, therefore the state of the house can deteriorate to an alarming degree before I notice. The second problem is that I live in fear that my friends may discover what my housekeeping reality really is.

Over the years I have had several very legitimate excuses presented to me by my friends to explain my lack of tidiness/cleanliness. "You have four children and work outside the home." True. "Your house is so tiny." This also is true. But they didn't know me when I lived in a much bigger house with NO kids. I was the same then as I am now, except I wasn't a quilter back then. Maybe I should have my DNA tested to see if I was born with a defective gene? Hmm ...

I've had many ideas on how to correct my hit and miss cleaning tactics. Several years ago, a friend recommended the book *Side Tracked Home Executives*. Excellent book. Great theory. Just the ticket! I spent days organizing my chores on index cards as they suggested. For a whole week I followed the plan. The next day I missed. So, I'm one day behind. So what? I'll catch up. I worked twice as hard the next day. Then life happened and I was week behind. End of that idea! It was a good program though.

My second solution, which has been more successful and which I am still using, is to invite someone over for coffee. I'm always amazed at how motivating that can be. This method is called for when we're in a particularly untidy state. I start by going outside, then entering the house through the mudroom. I want to see the house as company would view it. Then I whirl into action. First, I pick up the largest items that are out of place, working down to the smaller items. That way, if I'm interrupted, the worst is out of the way.

Maybe I've been going about this problem the wrong way. Instead of using up valuable time trying to meet some unattainable cleaning standard, perhaps I should concentrate on lowering the standard. Just think of all the extra time we'd all have if we didn't aspire to picture perfect homes with sparkling bathroom faucets! I'm going to advocate that we use sawdust on our floors and to shovel out once every three months or so. Friends, are you with me?

"Keeping house is like threading beads on a string with no knot on the end."
- Unknown

The Non-Gift Gift

There is a small box in the top drawer of my sewing cabinet that contains all the teeth from our four kids, collected by The Tooth Fairy in our house over the years. This collection gives my daughter Jen the willies. The grim array of slightly blood-tinged incisors, molars and front dentition sets her teeth on edge. (Did you catch my pun?)

A few months ago, I began making children's resin jewelry, as part of my crafting compulsion and the need to add fresh products into my online Etsy shop. I was embedding all sorts of doodads into silicone molds and topping them with the magical, clear acrylic liquid: Lego, pennies, buttons, tiny trolls, yellow duckies — whatever minute treasures crossed my path.

My tooth-phobic daughter had a birthday coming up and it occurred to me I could play a naughty trick on her by implanting one of the dreadful gum stumps into a resin pendant for her. I am rarely a prankster, but relished her anticipated look of horror when she realized the delicate looking necklace entombed her worst nightmare.

It came to the day before her birthday and I hadn't started to work the dastardly, horrifying present yet. An unbidden, but clear idea exploded into my consciousness. The non-gift was born. Instead, I presented my daughter with the following hand-written note enclosed in an appropriate gift box:

> Dear Jenny,
>   You are the first recipient of my new concept called the "Non-Gift Gift." I am NOT giving you a custom resin necklace with your first lost tooth that the Tooth Fairy has saved all these 36 years, for this very occasion.
>   You are welcome.
>   Love, your weird
>   momom

The next day, when I presented this unique non-gift to my Birthday Girl, the revulsion that briefly passed over her face while reading the enclosure was worth all the brain cells I burned up while concocting this crazy idea. She realized she'd had a close call and was grateful she didn't have to feign gratitude for the gruesome gift she almost received.

I expect many other people in my life will be getting non-gifts in the future. Each non-gift will be different, depending on their fears and trepidation. Much thought will be put into these imaginary non-presents.

P.S. Don't feel sorry for Jenny. I followed up the surprise non-gift with an envelope with an appropriate card and sheaf of bills to spend on her upcoming holiday.

Happy Ending (so you don't worry while reading)

Was there ever a more anticipated, fussed over, angst-ridden dress than the one my daughter needed for her most important day? Wedding you ask? No. High school graduation.

Jen requested that I make it. Being a romantic (and quite frugal), I agreed. Being a seamstress of some 30 years, I felt equal to the task. Do you feel some foreboding at this point? You should.

One fateful day in November we trotted off to our local fabulous fabric emporium. I thought this would be the most difficult portion of the dress construction. Wrong. Within half an hour we had chosen fabric and agreed on a pattern. Piece of cake. We were way ahead of schedule.

As I was taking the fabric out of the bag at home, I started having misgivings about our "perfect dress" choice. The fabric, a gorgeous ice blue, seemed too filmy. It had the texture of satin but was very cobwebby. A shiver of impending doom trickled down my spine. The procrastination had started.

After Valentine's Day, the pressure was starting to build. I was able to delay by declaring I couldn't cut out the dress until I had my scissors sharpened. That bought me only three days.

Much soul searching and pride swallowing resulted in my asking Jen if we could call in a professional. Enter MY mom, dressmaker extraordinaire. Gran would be pleased to help. She was transported from Union Bay in March to begin the task. I was to supervise.

The dress was cut out very efficiently and construction began. Immediately we ran into our first construction delay. The organdy which was to be set into the bodice neckline became stretched beyond recognition during the little handling it received after cutting. We had a construction huddle and it was quickly decided to switch to the alternative neckline. This

16

necessitated cutting out a an entirely new bodice. Did we have enough fabric left?

Nervous moments passed as we positioned and re positioned the pattern pieces. The only way they fit was upside down. The pattern on the fabric was very subtle. We took a chance Jen wouldn't notice. (She is finding out only now, as she reads this.) Mothers must deceive, if only rarely, to save face, money, sanity or all three.

Construction proceeded quickly after that nerve-racking start. Magically, it was all done except the hem and zipper. My Mom had to return home before Jen could do a final fitting. I popped in the invisible zipper and whipped up the hem. It was over, right? Wrong. Jen tried on the dress and the right side of the neckline buckled. Several frantic phone calls ensued. No solution presented itself.

My mother begged to be able to send money to buy a dress. "No!" I insisted. Too much time, money and effort had been expended. There had to be a way! It was only the first of April. We still had two months!

Jen solved the puzzle by tucking the sleeves down under her arms, making it a sleeveless gown. It went from being a sweet fairy-princess dress with puffed sleeves to a sophisticated gown suiting the young lady she'd become.

A few complicated alterations followed. My grade 12 tailoring teacher would have been proud. I complemented the gown with a matching drawstring bag and a chiffon shawl. Sounds like I'm drawing this story to a close, doesn't it? I think you can handle one more minor mishap.

The night before the prom, I had to do a minor adjustment on one of the spaghetti straps. I took it off the wire coat hanger it was hanging on and noticed rust marks on the straps where they had touched the hanger. At this point, I went into denial. I couldn't replace the straps, as I had no cording left. I tried spot cleaning, to no avail.

Jen is also learning this only now: I decided to ignore the rust stains and hope Jenny didn't see them, as they would be on her skin side.

As with so many things in our life, the prom was great. Many pictures were taken of the beautiful girl in THE dress, with her date, friends and family and we are left with good memories— without the rust stains. And thanks to Gran for her expertise and love.

(The dress prior to the bodice change)

(The following two tales were written one month apart for publication in 1999 in our local newspaper: "Metchosin Muse".)

Miracle at Metchosin Elementary

OK, maybe "miracle" is too strong a word. Perhaps a refreshing realization is closer to the truth. Let me explain.

In the beginning, there was a 40ish, matronly Mom who one day, unexpectedly, had a rib go out. For those who have never experienced this physical phenomenon, let me put it into perspective. I've had four children and childbirth doesn't touch this for pain! My neighbour, Todd, who drove me to the doctor (I couldn't drive for my tears) wanted to take me directly to the emergency room, as he was certain I was having a heart attack.

My very compassionate family physician diagnosed my problem and fixed me up promptly. After regaining my composure, I queried him as to what had caused this unpleasant physical situation. He patiently explained that I was overweight, I had no muscles, and I slouched! Personally, I like a doctor who doesn't lie.

Eight months and one more rib out incident transpired. I was forced to take my first move towards responsibility for my physical health. First, I joined Weight Watchers. Excellent program. I lost 15 pounds.

My second positive step, which is what this story is about, was to join the low impact aerobics class in the Metchosin elementary school gym. Having started countless other classes in the past— the operative word here is STARTED — I had little hope for success. I have never enjoyed exercise and have more excuses for not exercising than my kids have for not cleaning their rooms.

I was pleasantly surprised to find that I enjoyed the first class. The combination of Marlene, our perky teacher, invigorating music, and the fact that the women attending had a similar background and ability to mine was uplifting. Nary a spandex outfit was to be seen!

An astounding realization came the evening of my fifth session. While I was waiting for the class to start, I found I was voluntarily bouncing up and down in anticipation of this exercise class. It hit me like the proverbial ton of bricks! I was finally getting a glimmer of the concept of connecting with my body — even enjoying the physical activity!

I haven't forsaken my family to train for the Olympics, but I am looking forward to the search for other physical activities I might enjoy. Get out there and move! If it happened to me, it can happen to you. Your ribs will love you for it!

"Housework can't kill you, but why take a chance."
– Phyllis Diller

Another Miracle

Ladies, you overwhelmed me! I admit I had an ulterior motive when I wrote my aerobics article for the January Muse: we needed a few more people for the Low Impact Aerobics Class. The class had 12 to 15 ladies before the article, and we now have 30 to 40 participants. Bravo! It is gratifying to see so many mother/daughter teams come out, too.

Besides my improved fitness level, increased energy, and maintenance of my weight loss, I can now do EIGHT push-ups. That is up eight from my previous total of zero.

For my second fitness project, I've taken up running. I am goal-oriented and need definite objectives to work towards. To that end, I've joined a team from our aerobics class to participate in the Garden City run on April 25. Nothing like just jumping into the fire, is there?

Running appeals to my naturally thrifty nature: no fees, no membership, and no class start times. A good supportive pair of runners and you're off. Don't get me wrong, it is not a piece of cake. I cannot run very far before I need to walk a bit. So, I've been thinking about how I can justify my slower pace. Here's my solution. I am going to incorporate some of my low-impact-exercise-moves into my running program.

When I'm winded, I'll cover my need to catch my breath by doing a couple of side lunges to the left, then a couple of lunges to the right, followed by two kickbacks. A bit more running, then several hoop shots, arm presses, and side-jacks. I think it will make for a more complete work out. Any idea what I can call this regimen? Jumpy Jogging, maybe?

I think I will work on my running style a bit, though. In the short time I've been trotting along William Head Road, I've had three incidents where people I didn't know stopped to offer me a ride. One of them was a B.C. Transit bus! Was it because I was running frantically and looked like I was trying to get somewhere? Or perhaps I don't dress like a professional runner?

Anyway, I have such a frenetic lifestyle that I tend to decide suddenly that I have a small slot of time in which to run. I then jog wearing whatever I happen to have on. My wardrobe hasn't stretched to include appropriate running attire yet. I'll be scouring the second-hand stores for bright, comfortable garments soon.

What's my next fitness project, you ask? Well, if I live through the Garden City 10K run, I'll be lobbying our new Metchosin Community House to organize some running and walking groups so I can flap my gums while I'm becoming fit.

Well, got to run!

> **"Don't you wish you could finish cleaning the house and just hit the 'save' button."**
> **- Unknown**

My Val Odyssey

The passing of Charles Schultz in February 2000,was essentially the demise of Charlie Brown. I've always identified with Charlie Brown (as a teenager my nickname was Charley) — not for his character, but for his looks. A round moon face with no distinguishing features. Nothing offensive but nothing memorable either.

As a child, I wished for freckles, curly hair or even glasses — something that stood out. By the time I became an adult I had favourably come to terms with my unremarkable looks and noticed a by-product of this indistinguishableness.

On a very regular basis, I've had people remark how much I look like their cousin, aunt, neighbour or bank teller. I became so used to this phenomenon that I wasn't really surprised when events unfolded as they did. My story lends credence to the theory that we all have a doppelganger, somewhere in the world. Little did I realize I'd end up just down the road from mine. I'll explain.

Several years ago, a fellow came through my grocery store work station and asked me if I had a sister named Val. Knowing only one Val, I asked if he meant Val Dunne and was astonished when he said yes. I replied, "No, my sister's name is Janine". Then it was his turn to be surprised. Val Dunne happened to be my daycare provider for our youngest son, Rudy.

Shortly after, I was mistaken for Val, Mark Dunne's Mom, by a lad at the elementary school. Another time a woman sat beside me at a school band concert and addressed me as Val. A man yelled "Hello Val" from a passing car. Just recently a cashier at the Metchosin Country Store mistook me for my friend, Val.

Five Val incidents. I had been reporting to Val these incidents, as they happened, and, although I know she believed me, I think she thought I was exaggerating a bit. She had never had a "Charmaine" experience to equal my "Val" episodes until the summer of 2001. Val was at a printing shop I used to frequent, where she struck up a conversation with the clerk. "How is your summer going?" the young lady inquired. Val explained that she ran a daycare, but she was taking the summer off. "What happened to the octopus?" the clerk questioned, referring to the smoked octopus business my partner and I had for several years. Nonplussed, just momentarily, Val replied, "You think I'm Charmaine!"

Finally, my stories were vindicated! We think it's amusing but understandably justified. We're of the same build and stature, have the same ready smile and similar short brown hair. Standing side by side, I don't think we are startlingly alike, but if you didn't know us well and hadn't seen the other for a while, I can understand the confusion.

What do you think?

(Val on left, author on right.)

24

Octopus Diving

Octopus diving? I'm just teasing you. This article is actually about cashiering, but, really, would you have started reading this if it had been entitled "cashiering"? If I tell you something, do you promise not to tell my family? I enjoyed my job. Yes — cashiering! At home I moaned and complained about going to work, but really, it was fun, and they paid me well, and appreciated me, and I was warm and dry.

Cashiering has worked well for me on several different levels. My own opinion of my intelligence level has improved since I trained for the job. I was able to absorb the enormous amount of information, including hundreds of four digit produce codes, that I was expected to master. Go ahead, ask me what the code for onions is. 4665. Good, huh?

The level of stress was excellent. I have been a telephone operator, a dental receptionist, and a medical claim service representative, and found them all to be much, much more anxiety ridden than my most recent long-term occupation. Very occasionally I dealt with a difficult customer, but mostly the members of the public treated me very well, and me, them. The best part about a stressful customer is that they were gone in five minutes and probably wouldn't affect my long-term future.

I alluded earlier to the entertainment factor of cashiering. This is not the "laugh a minute" kind of situation, but rather a shared amusement type of interchange; for example, shared observances on the eating capacity of teenage boys (never mind the teenagers — yesterday my seven-year-old ate four pieces of toast and two pancakes for breakfast, and they were BIG pancakes at that!) I specialized in short clips about my family. If you had come through my work station often enough, I'd probably have told you a story you've heard before — I apologize in advance.

My job also afforded me the opportunity to gather cooking and eating tips on a wide variety of new ingredients: halva, lemongrass, longans, jicama, etc. I sometimes offered advice on foods my customers might not be familiar with like wheat berries, asiago cheese, sunchokes, and tofu. My favourite tofu tip: Shake and Bake, any flavour, on fingers of extra firm tofu. My kids liked the Honey Garlic flavour best. I came up with that myself. It kind of epitomizes my cooking style in those harried days: health married to convenience. You know: spinach and tuna thrown into a pot of Kraft dinner. Delicious!

Cashiering was also good exercise. I didn't need to go to the gym. After packing and hoisting a huge number of bags into shopping carts, who's got the energy?

I hope this gives you a better understanding of a cashier's day and hope none of you out there is quitting law school to become a cashier. I'm sure that the people-watching in law court is as good as it was in my grocery store. And again, I'm sorry again for leading you astray about the topic, but maybe I can make it up to you. I'll try to persuade my partner, Pete, who is an octopus diver, to write you a short piece about his workday.

Am I forgiven?

Neighbours

It was a beautiful spring morning in March, 1989 and I was in a bedroom, busy unpacking boxes from our recent move from the city to our new rural environs. Needing a coffee break, I headed for our kitchen. Rounding the corner, much to my amazement, I found myself gawking at a large goat that was munching compost out of a bucket, hooves on the counter, no less!

Having no livestock experience, I had no idea how to proceed. Was it dangerous? Would it bite me? I was sure it belonged to my new neighbours, but how should I get it back to its field? Think, think!

Goats eat anything, right?! I grabbed a box of snack crackers and began feeding them to the goat, while walking backwards. The goat, Buttons by name, I was to find out, was happily eating my crackers at quite a fast rate; and following me outside, and around to the gate joining our two properties. My crackers ran out at about the same time I deposited Buttons back into her own field. Whew! It was to be the first of many times that we fed Buttons and her field mates: horses and goats, deriving many hours of entertainment for my children and me.

After several days' recovery from my harrowing goat encounter, I bravely set off across Button's field with chocolate chip cookies in hand. Answering my door knock, Kathy came to the door, horrified that I was coming to her with cookies and not vice versa! I explained that I had observed her boys playing in the yard and that they seem to be of similar age to our kids. A fast friendship ensued all around.

Several weeks later, Kathy invited the neighbourhood ladies over for tea to introduce me to our corner of Metchosin. We had so much fun that afternoon that we decided to get together every week and our Breakfast Club was born. It was our steadfast weekly event until many of us went to work full time when our kids became older.

I love our neighbourhood! We borrow and barter kitchen utensils and ingredients. We watch each other's kids, feed each other's kids, drive each other's kids. We celebrate new jobs, congratulate on graduations and commiserate losses.

One of my neighbours gave me a fridge magnet that says it all: "Neighbours are friends nearby". If you haven't met your neighbour yet, get out your cookie sheet and start baking — and don't forget crackers for the goats!

(Mike feeding the neighbour's goats.)

My Dirty Little Secret

As we get older, I have observed that we become more like ourselves — truer to our true nature. What if you realized that your real self were less than socially acceptable? This is where I found myself recently, and it was an uncomfortable reality to digest.

My realization came slowly and, coincidentally, while trying to organize my sewing room and clean out the attic simultaneously, through the Christmas season. The attic needed some work done on it and had to be totally cleared out. We didn't have a basement for storage and the garage isn't weatherproof as a household cache. As some of the attic treasures were sewing oriented, it made sense to integrate them into the existing sewing room.

The room of sewing delights was already 25% over capacity, so there were boxes and bags everywhere you looked. This would make most people crazy, but I was as happy as a clam (how happy are clams, anyway?) Why isn't this a problem for me?

My adult children have been half joking about doing a hoarder's intervention with me. This started me thinking — was I a hoarder? No. Real hoarders save dumb stuff like plastic bags and newspapers. My collection was all useful items. Buttons, fabric, patterns, yarn, zippers, craft supplies — all essentials for making beautiful things, such as quilts or bow ties, warm bags and cooling collars, therefore I can't be a hoarder.

So what am I? I contemplated this and decided to look at other areas of my life for clues in order to peg my character. First was my work life. Part of my responsibility at Save On Foods was working at the Customer Service desk. I was happiest working on a Saturday afternoon when the phone was ringing, the line-up of patrons was long and cashiers needed directions. Pandemonium!

What about my social life? Here, again, I was contented when I had lots of projects on the go — classes to attend, coffee dates with friends, birthday parties to plan and vacations to look forward to. Heaven!

What did my alone time at home look like on a day off? The radio would be chattering away, the phone ringing, supper cooking, bow ties requiring completion and mailing away, and the dog would need walking. I'd be ecstatic.

What did all this information tell me? Chaos! I love and thrive on chaos — physical and mental. What is the opposite of obsessive-compulsive? Chaos.

Now you know my dirty little secret. Thanks for being part of it.

Family Dinners

As time passes, I'm finding family dinners more complicated than they used to be. In the olden days, a family dinner might consist of roast chicken, potatoes, two veggies and dessert. Those were the days, my friend, we thought they'd never end. We were wrong!

Nowadays I feel like a military leader going into an uncertain battle situation. Logistics, advance planning, shopping and cooking. All this after I determine the guest list. The usual invited guests number 12, me included.

Among these 12, there are seven different diets to work around. The general idea is to try to meet the eating requirements of each guest.

Here are the seven categories to cook around:

1.   There are two plant based eaters who don't eat any animal products.

2.   There's one ovo lacto vegetarian who will eat eggs and dairy.

3.   One person follows an anti-inflammatory diet to help with her arthritis pain. There are many "can consume" and "don't consume" component parts to that particular program, but I have her list memorized.

4.   We have two people who will eat everything and they're super easy. Having said that, one of these will tolerate only one food at a time on his plate.

5. Very curiously, two people have no sense of taste or smell, as they lost these two senses due to head injuries. Two separate accidents, though. These two sound easy but neither will eat anything they'd never tried before their accidents. So, no avocados, jicama or hearts of palm. Or sorghum, millet or kumquats.

6. Then me. I am the most difficult as I follow the Daily Dozen program. Dr. Michael Greger of nutritionfacts.org is my nutritional guru. No animal products, oil, salt or sugar, to name

the most difficult aspects of his fact-based regimen. I feel so much better on this eating routine and know my health is worth the extra effort but, yes, it's really hard to do for the first six months!

7.   The unknown category or, rather, the ever vacillating contingent are our two granddaughters. Their tastes change from one meal to the next. The quinoa they loved at their last shared meal might be the converse at this meal. Their tastes are always in flux.

As you can see, I have my work cut out for me when planning an eating procedure at our house. I doubt this is much different than many households these days. So many people have gluten sensitivities, lactose intolerance problems and moral beliefs around food.

None of the above is complaining or whining. I am very grateful to have all these terrific people in my life, a terrific partner who likes to cook with me, and the resources to feed them all!

I am grateful every day.

It's a Small World

We all have a similar story. Everybody has at least one.

It was 1985, and we were renting a town house in a 50-unit complex. This assemblage, like many of its kind, was peopled with many young couples with youngsters, who lived there while scraping up the down payment for their house.

Before long, my family had made the acquaintance of many of the children and their parents, owing to the green space in front of our complex. A favourite frolicking place, the park-like setting was a great way to meet the preschool set.

One of the first people I met was a happy young mum named Ingrid, and her little daughter, Katy. When I meet people for the first time, if they have a noticeable maritime accent, I ask from where they originally hail. Ingrid was from Halifax. The conversation went on to include the fact that her husband, Paul, was from a small village that I surely would never have heard of, on Prince Edward Island. As my mother was born and raised on PEI and I spent eight years there as a child, I speculated that I may have heard of his village.

After a little back and forth banter, I elicited the fact that he was from North Rustico. You might have already guessed this: my mother was from North Rustico, too! Not only were they from the same village, but further investigation by my mother uncovered the fact that Paul was her second cousin. Small world!

My next example of this phenomenon originated in the same housing complex. The young mother involved in this story was a next-door neighbour, Lynn. Our kids played together almost every day. Lynn and I shared many cups of tea, as well as lots of personal history.

When we had known each other for a year, Lynn asked me to babysit her son while she went to her grandmother's funeral. I went to collect her son, and get the details as to where she might be located, in case of emergency. After the service, she

33

was going to a reception at her aunt's and uncle's house. She looked up their number in the telephone directory (no Google available back then).

"Here's the number" Lynn said, pointing to an H. Welch, on Crease St. in Victoria. Amazingly, she was pointing to my uncle Harold's phone number. "That's my aunt and uncle!" I blurted. Uncle Harold and Aunt Jeanette.

"No, that's my aunt and uncle" said Lynn.

After the dust settled, we agreed that they were aunt and uncle to both of us. Uncle Harold was my father's brother, and Aunt Jeanette was Lynn's mother's sister.

All that time we had known each other and didn't know we were related, however distant the connection. I wonder if there is a name for our relationship status.

Small world! And a wondrous world, at that!

> "Cleaning with children around is like shoveling during a blizzard."
> – Margaret Culkin Banning

Placebos and Functional Foods

I'll let you in on another one of my guilty little secrets: I am an addict of nutraceuticals and vitamin supplements.

Several friends and relatives have harangued me for years about this (possibly) expensive habit. Their attitude has been that the nutraceuticals are an unnecessary waste of money. Apparently we can get all of our nutrients from our food. APPARENTLY.

The Merriam-Webster Dictionary defines nutraceutical: "a foodstuff (as a fortified food or a dietary supplement) that is held to provide health or medical benefits in addition to its basic nutritional value — also called functional food".

We could debate the pros and cons of supplements indefinitely, but we won't, not now, anyway. Read on. What I do want to discuss is a mind-blowing concept I've just recently read about. It explains my obsession with vitamins and their ilk.

A placebo can work even when you know it's a placebo. Harvard Medical School describes open label placebos as treatment that the patients understand are sugar pills. The placebo response effect can work for conditions such as chronic low back pain, fatigue, nausea or depression. This is amazing information by itself.

The second bit of recently acquired info is the discovery of a placebo gene. This explanation, in addition to the previous revelation, describes me perfectly. I know I have this gene. Imagine: to believe in placebos and be rewarded by them with results is fantastic!

The concerned people in my life who thought I was gullible may now rest easy. With my newly realized placebo super powers, I am pretty much bulletproof health-wise.

Now, please excuse me. I have several handsful of supplements to gobble down before supper.

Knit Fit

There will soon be a new exercise craze sweeping through the nation and I'm giving you the chance to be ahead of the wave. As I conceived the concept, I have named it "Knit Fit". Fit, as in physically fit, not fit as in convulsions. Knit Fit is a rare opportunity to mix relaxation and exercise. How is this possible, you ask? Basically, you are walking and knitting at the same time. How cool is that?

What is Knit Fit's history? The idea hit me about the same time that I got back into knitting. Many good ideas spring from necessity, as did this one. My large, blonde Pyrenees-cross dog, Sally, needed her daily exercise, and I wanted to knit. I was knitting apple cozies (draw-string covers that cushion fruit in lunch bags), items that requires no stitch counting, and that are knit in the basic garter stitch, so I decided to marry the two activities. Ta-da! Much to my delight, and Sally's, I get projects knitted and she gets to gambol.

This is what I do: I sling one of my long-handled totes over my shoulder, with my yarn issuing from it, knitting needles in hand, and a simple knitting pattern in my head, I am off and walking/ knitting. Oh, of course, Sally's leash is adorning my left wrist. (She is very good about not pulling.)

If you don't own a dog, you could invite a friend to accompany you, which would accomplish another need: socialization. I'm starting to think this Knit Fit is the answer to a lot of small quandaries. We now have exercise, relaxation and socialization wrapped up in one procedure.

A few suggestions, though: it is safer to walk on a clear trail, such as the Galloping Goose (our local walking trail), that affords terrific visibility and no vehicular traffic to interrupt your concentration: Spring, Summer and Fall are the best seasons to Knit Fit, as trying to knit while wearing mitts is rather awkward.

Can you crochet while walking? Yes, but it would be called Crochet Fit, which, I'm sure you'll agree, doesn't have the cachet of Knit Fit.

Mandy, my friend and Jazzercise instructor, was worried when she first heard about this new regimen. Fear not, sweet lady, Knit Fit it is not a substitute for Jazzercise. It isn't the ideal all-round workout, just an enjoyable adjunct to it.

Even as you are reading this, I am loading my tote with some Salvation Army-found yarn and I'm off to enjoy this fabulous spring weather in our beautiful environs. Arent we smart to live here?

(Apple Cozy)

Lousy Love

Want to hear my lousy love story? Why lousy? Because the lice involved invoke a warm fuzzy feeling inside me, to this very day.

This tale happened in 1962 and began in grade 2 during printing practice. As I was concentrating on forming legible letters, I scratched my head. To my surprise, and incredibly, to my delight, a small sesame seed-sized bug appeared on my page. I remember showing my friend who sat behind me, marveling at its magical appearance out of thin air.

When I returned home that afternoon, I reported this mystical occurrence to my mom. She seemed more annoyed than entranced with this bug's arrival on my desk.

Thus began the daily evening ritual of lice removal from my scalp. After Mom put my three younger siblings to bed, we would go into our sparsely furnished living room for my manual lice and nit removal process. Are you feeling itchy yet?

If you have never been blessed with lice, you may need a bit of explanation on the different treatments used to get rid of these tiny, itch-inducing critters. Nowadays, a strong insecticidal shampoo-type method is used in conjunction with a very fine comb to deal with the nits, which are the lice eggs.

Back in the dark ages, in the time this story is set, there were no magic potions or fancy hair gizmos to help. It took painstaking and time-consuming labour to remove the quick-moving, translucent lice and the tiny, white, oval-shaped nits.

My hair was blonde in those days, which wasn't the best colour for ease of lice detection. Lice show up better against darker hair, as do the nits, which are glued onto the hair shafts near the scalp.

Here is the tricky part: it is best to try to eradicate as many lice and their eggs as soon as possible, to prevent the proliferation and spread of these nearly indestructible nuisances. This necessitates daily scrutiny because nits take six to nine days to hatch.

OK, OK, enough of the creepy crawly bug talk. Where is the love connection? My mom was never a lovey-dovey, touchy-feely mother. Quite the opposite. My lizard brain quickly connected me sitting on the floor with my head settled between my Mom's knees with a warm, cozy feeling. I came to associate the nightly head grooming with parental love. Having my mother's undivided attention and having her focusing only on me was nirvana!

Although our Mom loved us and showed her love other ways, I now know the absence of physical touch had a profound effect on my confidence growing up.

This story wasn't easy to write. I hope I have been a more demonstrative mother, and that my children don't have to rely on memories of lousy love!

> "A spotless house is a sign of a misspent life."
> - Unknown

My Twilight Zone Moment

This otherworldly tale centres on Rhonda Byrne's book and reinforcement program called *The Secret*.

Do you know this theory, very popular quite a few years ago? I first heard about the unlikely notion from my best friend and my oldest son, within 24 hours of each other. I have always believed in signs, and this seemed to be a definite signal that I should investigate this very popular concept. The clincher really was that both parties had the DVD version of the book, but when I asked to borrow it, they both said no, without hesitation! They both insisted that they needed to watch it again and again.

So, I bought the CD version, as I prefer to listen to audio books as I go about my day.

Very soon, I was being mesmerized by Rhonda's melodic Australian voice. The basic idea of *The Secret* is the Law of Attraction. What you're thinking is what you will attract to you. You can have health, wealth and happiness. Or the flip side of the coin is that if you think negatively, you will attract negative occurrences. This is described in different ways, with lots of examples, on the CD.

OK, I know I'm very gullible, but even I was skeptical of this whole idea. I felt this was very weird — too much like voodoo.

As intriguing as the whole idea was, I felt foolish trying it out. I was ready to shelve this peculiar program under the heading of "Not Anytime Soon." I quickly put it out of my mind.

Carrying on with my life, *The Secret* CD landed in my give-away pile. Two days later, I had to be at work for my 5:00 a.m. price-change shift. I awoke with my right eye running profusely. The tears seemed to be burning my super sensitive eyes. At work, the condition was very irritating, and the thought that was running in a loop through my brain was that I wanted — no, I NEEDED — an eye patch to cover my light-sensitive eye.

At 9:00 a.m. (that was my meal break), I planned to go to the walk-in clinic and have the doctor diagnose my problem. For an hour I thought only of this one idea. I needed an eye patch. I wanted an eye patch. I wished for an eye patch. I was crouched down on the floor, placing a label on a bottom shelf, when I glanced up and saw a plastic eye patch hanging on a display case. I was gobsmacked! This wasn't anything we had ever sold in the store. It was a promotional product for the *Pirates of the Caribbean* video and I had never seen it before!

What was I to think now?

Well, I did the only thing that made any sense. I have harnessed this amazing power and have created a mantra for myself that I have used for more than 20 years and it goes like this:

> I am happy.
> I am healthy.
> I am wealthy.
> I am tall.

You are probably wondering how is it working for me.
Well, two out of four ain't bad!

Inspiration

All these stories I write are true stories, generally based on my personal experiences. The next two stories were told to me by a couple of colourful characters who were the main protagonists. The critter in the first story survived, but, unfortunately, the second creature didn't. Tender-hearted readers should stop reading after the first tale is completed.

My friend, Amanda, having dropped in on her parents for a quick visit, but noticing that time was getting on, said her farewells. Going to the door and finding one of her shoes missing, she knew the teeny Yorkie, Ratty, who ruled the house, had removed it to one of her lairs.

This was a common occurrence, but Amanda didn't have the time or the inclination to play "keep away" with the dog that day. Several futile efforts to separate dog and shoe ensued, as the four-pound dynamo had a death grip on her expensive leather footwear.

Glancing around, inspiration struck and Amanda sprang into action. Scooping up the dog and attached shoe, she moved quickly to the chest freezer and deposited both canine and shoe into its frosty depths.

It took 30 seconds for the diminutive pup to relinquish her leather treasure.

Amanda never again had shoe wars with Ratty. I believe the tiny canine went off shoes entirely after that.

Rita is the combatant in the second saga. A brief encounter with her in a consignment store elicited the story of this fantastical event. A fisherman friend of Rita phoned her one evening to arrange a drop-off of a small octopus he had caught as a bycatch that day. He would leave it on her porch early the next morning.

On rising, our heroine, Rita, carried the green garbage bag containing the seafood gift to the sink and upended the bag. To her immense horror, the 10-pound octopus that tumbled out of the bag was ALIVE! Rita certainly wasn't prepared to do arm-to-arm-to-arm armed combat with the mollusk, now ecstatic that it had been released from its plastic bag prison.

YIKES! With the children soon to be mobbing the kitchen looking for their breakfasts, Rita had to act quickly. A half-hearted attempt to return the octopod back into its garbage bag jail failed miserably.

Grabbing a meat cleaver, she chopped ineffectually at the confused sea creature's appendages. This didn't slow down the hapless critter in the least.

Understanding the futility of the knife strategy, Rita cast her eyes around the kitchen for another solution. Much like my friend Amanda, she spied the freezer.

Propping the lid open, she gathered the future dinner main course onto a cookie sheet and deposited it in the frigid interior.

That probably wasn't the most humane way of dispatching the unlucky sea dweller, but was less traumatic than it being slowly hacked to death.

Inspiration. You never know when you might need it.

The Best Teenage Rebellion

It was 1995. I came home from work one evening to find our 14-year-old daughter, Jenny, bawling her eyes out in her bedroom. Being a very down to earth, sensible and mature teenager, I was shocked to find her in a nearly hysterical state. Over and over I queried as to what was wrong? Why was she crying? What had happened to upset her so much?

She managed to calm down enough to choke out that she had done something I had told her not to do, and then she started crying even harder.

Now I was fighting hysteria. Was she pregnant? Had she become hooked on heroin? Had she murdered someone?

These thoughts were flying around in my head, but my mothering instinct stayed calm. I uttered a few calming phrases like "I will always love you no matter what" and "We can get through this together". She managed to pull herself together long enough to utter the most wonderful phrase ever: "Mom, I shaved my legs".

The relief that swept over me was marvelous! It was all I could do not to laugh out loud! The emotional release from the very long 10 minutes of parental angst was something I will remember always.

Realizing that this had been a very real moral dilemma for Jenny, I had to think quickly about how to respond. My retort was that the results of the shaving would be its own punishment. I had originally told Jen she didn't need to shave, as her legs weren't hairy. This incident was the only infraction Jenny ever committed against my wishes. To say she was a dream teenager would not be an exaggeration.

I am one proud momma.

What, Me Worry?

There was a time, a long while past, when I would fret about little, everyday things. A friend being late for an engagement would leave me feeling harried and frustrated. Had they forgotten? Had they had an accident? Should I do something?

The remedy for this pointless type of "stewing" began with the birth of my first child. Being anxious that I should know all there was to know about what was good for my daughter, I picked up Dr. Spock's book *Baby and Child Care*. I started reading, and by the time I made it to page 87 I was a wreck! All the illnesses that my baby could contract? Or life-threatening situations she might get into? How was I to protect her from all these potentially deadly happenings? Wrap her in plastic? Move to an isolated mountaintop?

My sensible mother told me to use the book as a reference, rather than a source of fodder for night-time terrors. I took a deep breath and never looked back. This served as an excellent general life lesson. It is always good to be prepared and not take unnecessary risks, but there will always be factors we cannot control. It is important to discern the difference between the two.

The other coping strategy I have developed over the years is to leave the worrying to the people around me. My father was, and still is, my main worry monger. His biggest nightmare was a possible break-in while he was away from home. Well, his nightmare became a reality several months ago. On returning from a trip to town he found, indeed, that someone had broken into his garage.

The extraordinary thing was that not only had someone broken in, but they had left a whole lot of stuff there too! At first, Dad thought my brother was responsible for the mass of sports equipment, suitcases and clothes that now occupied the centre of the workshop. The quirky details were the $20 bill and two chocolate bars perched on top of this pile. A quick phone call eliminated ownership by my bachelor sibling.

On closer inspection, a luggage tag revealed the true owner of the abandoned masculine jetsam. The name and address were totally unknown to Dad or to anyone else in our family. After puzzling over the dilemma, Dad called the listed number. The woman who answered the call was equally mystified. After Dad gave her a detailed description of the accumulated items, she concluded that her husband had cleared out his personal belongings and had left without telling her!

To this day, we have no clue as to why the fellow chose my father's garage to park his treasures, or whether he ever intended to return to claim them. The two men lived 25 miles apart and had never heard of each other. With no comment, the wife came and collected the discarded possessions that same day, so I guess we will never know.

What this situation proved to me was that, as much as Dad had worried about being broken into, it did not prevent it from happening. Dad returned the money but shared the chocolate bars with us. We figured the guy was paying Dad rental storage with the $20.

These days, my husband and daughter do most of the worrying that needs to be done daily.

As my friend Bob Marley says: "Don't worry, be happy".

Oven Peeling

Oven cleaning is one of those jobs most effectively executed when the mood hits me. For my oven's sake, it's too bad the mood hasn't hit for some time. Time has a funny way of slipping by. When WAS the last time I cleaned the oven anyway? Maybe I could figure out how long ago it was by counting the layers of foil on the bottom. What foil? You know: the aluminum foil you put down to make it easier to clean the next time.

Hmm. There are several layers here, but they seem to be stuck together. I probably shouldn't have thrown a clean layer of foil on top of the dirty one. Two or three times. Maybe four times. And it seems to be stuck to the bottom of the oven in several places. Melded on, actually. It looks pretty bad! I've noticed dinner guests sneaking peeks into the oven to check out the dinner and trying to stifle looks of horror at the spectacle inside (the dirty oven being the spectacle, not my dinner).

Maybe I'll skip the whole procedure and take the route my husband used back in his bachelor days: when his stove/oven became too bad, he'd take it to the dump and replace it with a second-hand oven. Expensive, but effective.

Wait! The phone is ringing. Guess what? My friend is getting a wall oven and wants to give us her self-cleaning oven. Bonus. No more tin foil. No more angst over cleaning the oven. I can throw out my special oven cleaning clothes. Orange velour never did become me.

It's now one year later, give or take a month. I am about to activate the self-cleaning oven for the first time. Horrors! My friend didn't leave me an instruction book. None of these knobs make sense to me. Twisting one, then another, results in no results. How can I possibly call her and admit that it's been a whole year and I haven't even spent the two minutes it takes to turn on the darn self-cleaning oven?

Google to the rescue! Friends and relatives: I now have the oven cleaning thing down pat. My fridge is cleaned regularly, and I change my dishcloths every day. Don't be afraid of eating here. I haven't lost a guest, yet.

The Christmas Gift

This story begins in mid December, some years ago. It was a Breakfast Club morning like many others. Maybe it was a bit more special as our dozen members were lunching at the Mychosen Cafe for our Christmas get together. I had no foreboding that anything extraordinary would happen — no niggling feeling that I was about to have a major shift in outlook — just pleasant anticipation of a congenial party with some classy, interesting women.

We had agreed among ourselves that a lunch at the restaurant would simplify our busy pre-Christmas lives. As a concession to the festive reason for our gathering, we thought handmade or inexpensive gifts could be exchanged without a lot of added stress. These wrapped offerings were piled in the middle of the table, none meant for anyone specifically.

After ordering our lunch and while waiting for its arrival, we each proceeded to choose a gift from the pile in front of us. The flat rectangular gift didn't beckon me especially, but I know now that it was there especially for me.

My gift opening was interrupted by a relative newcomer to our group, who was anxious to explain the origin of her gift. My new friend, Vio, short for Violaine, had been working with a group of teenage girls from a rag picking community in Cairo, Egypt. This community supported themselves with the proceeds of their combing of the city dumps for clothing they could sell for rags. My new companion had been working with these young girls to try to add value to the fabric that was salvaged from the castoff clothing by reconstructing these bits into saleable items[1]. This gift, carried from the other side of the world (both physically and socially) was a sample of their efforts.

---

[1] Here is the contact info for the online store that promotes the products for the Zabbaleen (garbage collectors): Https://zabbaleenproducts.com

After hearing this compelling story, I carefully removed the wrapping with considerably more interest than I had begun with. In my friend's voice I heard a desire for me to understand this offering and a need for it to touch me.

I unwrapped two place mats and was awestruck. These mini quilts were sewn with what appeared to be vintage cottons of some considerable age and questionable quality. Done in a sort of hodgepodge, crazy quilting style, the dominant colour was red. Not fashionable, not artistic, and definitely not "pretty".

These quilted efforts profoundly touched a chord in me. I am a quilter who mostly works with "found" fabric that I recycle from our castoff clothing or discover in my second-hand stores' hoards. I have always had a need to recycle seemingly useless items into something serviceable, and red is my favourite colour.

The tenuous connection I felt with those girls, this ability to turn old and discarded clothes into usable housewares, was perhaps the only thing we had in common. A half a world away, I couldn't begin to imagine their daily lives or living conditions, their hopes or their dreams.

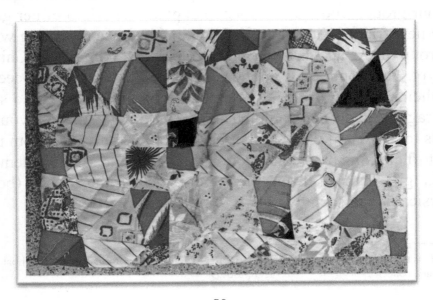

This place mat (the hamster ate the second one) will serve as a reminder to me of the privileged life we live and help me appreciate my chosen lifestyle. When I want to grumble about my tiny kitchen, or moan about the lack of leisure expenditures, I'll look at the place mat and be glad that me and mine are warm, dry, fed and healthy. My friend gave me thankfulness for Christmas. That is the BEST Christmas gift there is.

Merry Christmas.

Puzzling

Do you ever wonder about the backstory of a puzzling occurrence? Here are three examples of recent inconsequential events that left me chuckling long afterwards.

Our recent Covid-19 pandemic effectively killed my 12-year-old bow tie business. With lock downs worldwide, who had anywhere to dress up for? With sanctions being lifted, I had been ruminating about winding down my neck accessory manufacturing and pivoting to other products.

While sorting through my bow tie supplies, I decided to pare down the quantity of bow tie clips. If I lived to be 100, I wouldn't put a dint in my cache. I put 20 in each of two zip lock bags and donated them to my favourite second hand charity.

A week to the day after that, I moseyed down to our farm stand to pick up a parcel from Amazon. On lifting up the package, I noticed a second bundle underneath. Puzzled, I opened that bag to reveal the two bags of bow tie hardware I had just sent out into the Universe. WHAT?

The enclosed note explained the clips were bought on the assumption that they were metal clothespins. On realizing that they weren't laundry hardware, and understanding their true purpose, the purchaser decided to donate them to someone who could use them. Can you guess who?

This anonymous person knew of my bow tie acumen, discovered where I lived, and kindly re-donated the clips back from whence they came. As the note wasn't signed, I hope the generous donor reads this and hears the thank-you implied in this article.

I took this incident as a strong indication that the Universe is convinced I should remain a creator of funky and fun shirt accessories.

The second puzzling event that happened recently occurred right here in our lovely Free Library at the Seniors' Centre. Just inside the door is an intake table where people drop off books and jigsaw puzzles.

I noticed the puzzle on top of the pile had a tiny bag and note taped onto the box cover. Inside the zip-lock bag was a solitary puzzle piece and the note explained that the lonely fragment did not belong to the attached jigsaw. Huh?

My mind was in a whirl! What did the well-meaning previous owner think was going to happen to that forlorn cardboard segment? As there are approximately 100 puzzles in the library, how could the proper "mother" puzzle ever be found, assuming that the sad orphan piece came from one of the resident puzzles warehoused at our beloved activity centre. My brain hurt thinking of all the possible ways to reunite this pathetic puzzle morsel with its fellows.

I came across a new word today that I think explains this paradox: problemize – to make into or regard as a problem requiring a solution.

As I was typing this fluff piece, I checked my Marketplace listing for the puzzle sales and discovered another crazy person who was advertising not one, but two, single puzzle pieces that needed homes. Of course they were free, but honestly!

What an obscure hobby: reuniting and making broken puzzles whole. I can't think anyone who takes on this pastime is ever going to be successful, but I could be wrong.

"Stand" by Me

Do you know what I like about Metchosin? In addition to the beauty, the great people and the sheep? The fact that someone would buy a $1.00 item from the stand at the bottom of our driveway and leave 67 cents, only to return the next day with the remaining 33 cents.

Originally, we set up the stand during daffodil season, to share our yellow bounty with our neighbours. My kids and I picked these harbingers of Spring, tied bunches of them with yarn and placed them in jam jar vases on an old, rickety wheelbarrow.

I was delivering several bunches to the stand one day when a customer queried why some bunches had 10 flowers while others had 16 stems. I explained that my six-year-old son, Rudy, must have been the bundler. With Rudy not being an accurate counter, there would be bonus bundles amongst the regular offerings.

Next, an old, formica kitchen table served as our stand, sporting a red tablecloth as an attractant for our wares. This second phase of "stand" marketing was brought about by our need for test marketing our new enterprise's products.

We needed some passive input for our future and found this method to be an excellent marketing technique. My mother-in-law explained its success as the no-pressure way to shop. Stuff is for sale but no one looks over your shoulder — no hard sell. Drop your money in the pot and tote your purchase away.

People ask if we worry about theft. Yes and no. We've lost more than one item, I but doubt very much the thief was a Metchosinite. I am developing a self-destructive mechanism that will make an item disappear if it's not paid for.

Out of necessity, we have developed a "stand" etiquette regarding money retrieval. Rudy, the generous bundler, was in charge of collection of the accumulated funds. When he saw a vehicle drive up, he would hurl himself out of the house and run pell-mell down the driveway. As often as not, the potential customer would pull away at the sight of my over enthusiastic money collector. He now waits a discreet minute AFTER the customer departs before plying his funds appropriation.

I have taken a page out of Rudy's playbook. From his example, I have worked exercise into my replenishing of the stand. Running to the stand saves time and will serve to put me into running shape sooner. So, come by, take a look, and keep me fit!

I didn't think I should use my Metchosin Muse goodwill to promote our business, so I won't tell you what we are selling. I'm not fudging or hedging you. You'll have to come to visit us on William Head Road. I'm "standing" for you.

(Our red farm stand)

"Cleaning with children in the house really is like brushing your teeth while eating Oreos."
— Phyllis Diller

Ready to Switch Gears

What a whirlwind were the two years of Covid-19 mask making. Here's the way it played out. As my partner Pete and I were in a "bubble" with his 90-year-old mother, Nan, our world was rather small.

Why did our self-imposed isolation preclude me keeping up with my friends by phone, as I would have in the "old days"? After ruminating on that for a while, I concluded that texting had taken over for vocal communication, and I was a painfully slow texter. The second factor was that we weren't going anywhere, doing anything or seeing anybody. What was there to talk about?

Very soon, I would be embroiled in the most absorbing and gratifying sewing experience ever. Early on we were told not to wear cloth masks. The general idea was that all masks should be funneled to the very essential health care workers, as they were on the front lines against this very scary pandemic. Disposable masks were as scarce as hen's teeth. My good friend and neighbour, Tracy, who is a terrific nurse, advised me to ignore the request NOT to sew cloth masks. She assured me we would all soon be wearing homemade cloth masks, and she was right.

The evolution of masks followed the availability of mask supplies. Initially elastic was impossible to source, as was black cotton fabric. The supposition was that both components were requisitioned by commercial mask makers. Due to my ongoing bow-tie-making business, I had enough of both items to be able to manufacture face coverings as fast as I could sew.

A short time into my mask making adventure, I realized I couldn't keep up with the demand. Even sewing eight or ten masks a day wasn't keeping up with the orders. As nothing else was happening in our lives, I could sew endlessly, but often had 10 to 14 day lag time between orders arriving and mask completion.

Enter my trusty sewing fanatic friend, Sandy Schull. As she had often helped me keep up with bow tie orders, she was ready and willing to use her exquisite sewing ability to aid my mask factory frenzy.

The fabulous side benefit of this frantic project was the ability for me to buy as much fabric as I wanted. The luxury of purchasing $400-$500 worth of gorgeous textiles each time I visited a fabric store was awesome! My stash grew and grew. My sewing room was increasingly becoming more chaotic by the month.

March of 2022 saw my orders dwindle to a slow trickle, as Covid restrictions began to lift and our previous existence started to look more possible. Thus ended two solid years of mask construction.

I was more than ready to change gears. What amazing sewing adventure await me next? I can hardly wait.

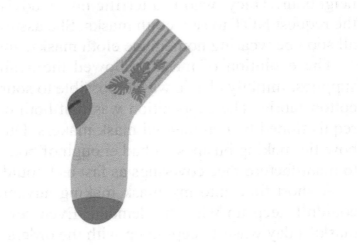

Of Underwear and Hearts

Need an attitude adjustment? Have a heart attack. It worked for me. February 4, 2014 to be exact. It was unexpected; I mean, really, do many people plan to have a heart event?

It was particularly unexpected, because the day before I had been given a two-thumbs-up bill of health via a complete medical. The doctor reported low blood pressure, low blood sugar and great cholesterol levels. He patted me on the shoulder as I left and said I was in really good shape for 58. The only prescription I took was Synthroid, for my low thyroid.

It was five days before my what was to be my first trip to Mexico. The last thing I was worrying about was my health. The most urgent thing on my mind was finding my funky sun hat I had stored somewhere last fall.

Around 11 a.m. I jumped into the car for a quick visit to the corner store. En route, in the space of three seconds, I experienced nausea, light headedness and a heavy weight on my chest. I knew the flu didn't present like that, but a heart attack wasn't even conceivable for my planned busy day. No pain was involved.

Not wanting to go home to an empty house, I drove to my wonderful and sensible friend and neighbour, Cathy Watson. Not liking my symptoms, or my pallor, she called 911. The emergency operator suggested I take aspirin while we waited for help to arrive. Cathy had Tylenol and Ibuprofen, neither of which would help thin my blood.

Stephanie, Ben and Gord, our awesome Volunteer Firefighters, must have been cruising down William Head Road when they received the call, because they seemed to materialize almost instantly. Cathy seemed relieved to be handing over my continued existence to these knowledgeable and practised individuals. Oxygen flowed and a medical history was taken. Ben was not going to let The Fudge Fairy die!

Just as my saviour was lifting my shirt to listen to my heart, I had an awful, terrible, horrible thought: I was wearing my old, ratty, pill-infested brassiere! And the bra was beige and the pills were red from wearing a new, fluffy-on-the-inside, sweatshirt. Horrors! Suddenly, that was all I could think about.

All thoughts of what was possibly happening inside my body, that maybe I was experiencing a heart attack and possibly wouldn't live until the afternoon, were gone. In their place was the absurd notion that by evening the whole of Metchosin would know of my slovenly undergarment.

My horror was interrupted by the arrival of three ambulance attendants and three advanced life support responders. Things were really swinging into high gear! Cathy had 10 people in her living room and I imagined they were all trying to ignore my grubby bust supporter. The mind plays amazing tricks to help us cope with stressful situations.

Just after being placed in one of the two ambulances, I began to shake violently. Not being content to have just a heart attack, my body decided to have a panic attack as well. Although my consciousness wanted to divert my attention away from the cruel reality of what was happening, a secondary awareness took over and then I was a real mess!

The very sweet man attending to me gave me some Gravol and a bit of Morphine to cope with my anxiety. PRESTO! I was no longer the least bit concerned about much of anything. I had never understood the allure of drugs — but now I do. That poor man had to listen to me blather on about bow ties all the way to the Royal Jubilee Hospital. I apologize, kind sir.

The 35-minute ride flashed by seemingly instantly, during which, through the magic of wires and machines and computers, it was determine I was experiencing a heart attack.

When we arrived at the emergency department, another crowd of ten people fussed over me, drawing blood and hooking up machines. This time one of my minders actually removed my shirt and the offending dingy breast underwear. Guess what. Some sort of premonition must have been running in the recesses of my mind that morning so I had put on a brand new bra. Nothing ratty about it at all. My reputation was saved!

At that moment I spied my crying daughter, Jenny, across the large department. My euphoria over the discovery of the new undergarment compelled me to fist pump into the air and yell "Jenny, I'm not gonna die!"

I was whisked away to undergo a painless angiogram that showed I had completely clear arteries, except for the one at the bottom of my heart, you know the one — where the heart's pointy end is located. The efficient technician inserted a medication into my vein which broke up the blockage. The problem was solved and resolved. No surgery was necessary, and for that I was thankful. The cardiologist had no explanation for the whole experience, but my hunch was that it was an infection-induced problem caused by a simmering, abscessed tooth and a fierce "Lady Town" infection.

I now walk to the store instead of drive, and eat much more healthfully. I still plan, some day, to make it to Mexico.

Seriously though, here are a couple of suggestions. (No, I won't nag you about your diet or those few extra pounds.) Always carry aspirin — not the coated type. If you suspect the possibility of a heart attack, chew two, don't swallow them whole. Call for help immediately if you have unusual symptoms. Heart attacks don't always present as chest-wracking pain. Always buy travel cancellation insurance (I didn't). And last, but not least, wear clean underwear. I did!

And Then ...

I thought I should correct a misconception you may have received from my last article, that my heart attack was all fun and games. It may have seemed to be a "laugh riot", what with the paramedics paying me all that attention, the VERY effective drugs, and the visitors bringing me gorgeous flowers. Those parts were great, but there were some repercussions I experienced which I hadn't anticipated.

After a month of reliving daily my most traumatic day, I woke up one morning and decided I was done with the shadow of my heart situation hanging over me. I declared myself over it. Done! Finished! Little did I know.

Several months after my fractious, memorable February 4, 2014 red-letter day, I underwent an echo cardiogram. I wasn't expecting anything of negative interest to be found when I was called by my doctor's office to go in to learn the results. When joking with the receptionist, I suggested my results were probably 100% and I would be coming in to hear positive news. Nope. She checked my chart and told me I had an aneurysm.

After hanging up the phone, I mentioned to our then 22-year-old son, Rudy, that I was going to Google this mysterious-to-me condition. His considered opinion was that no good would come of my inquiry to the computer gods. As it was two days before I was to confer with Dr. O'Connor, my curiosity got the upper hand.

Moments after booting up my computer tablet, I went running to Rudy's room, shouting "I shouldn't have looked it up!"

It turned out that there are many possible severities of these silent killers. Let the nail biting begin! Long story made shorter, my aneurysm was a result of the heart tissue dying in the spot where the attack happened, at the bottom of my ticker. It isn't a large aneurysm and shouldn't be a problem — probably ...

The next incident to occur was my frozen shoulder. Again, it was a result of my heart malfunction. No fun. Quite painful. Lots of chiropractor visits. You should definitely skip this after effect, if you have a choice!

At the six-month mark, post heart attack, I was quite confident that I was on top of my health situation. I happened to be walking on the side of our road when a life support ambulance screamed past me, with all lights flashing and sirens blaring. I immediately burst into tears, instantly reliving my harried ride into the Victoria Jubilee Hospital. It seemed I hadn't recovered emotionally yet.

Lastly, after a year or so post heart attack, I endured an allergic reaction to the Ramipril, the high blood pressure medication that I had been prescribed (even though I didn't have high blood pressure). As I have always had very low blood pressure, my belief is that my body was rebelling against this ill-considered drug. The awful response resulted in half my tongue swelling up with Bubonic Plague-looking sores on my swollen tongue tissues. Painful doesn't describe it!

The only good thing that came out of that situation was the four pounds I lost while being able only to sip only tepid liquids through a straw placed as far back on my tongue as I could comfortably place it.

Mostly, now, I wake up and try and squeeze in as much living as I can each day, mindful that it's a precious gift, this thing we call life.

Enjoy! I do.

Letting Go

It's natural; it's normal. I knew it would happen some day. I had prepared myself accordingly. So what was the problem, I asked myself?

You have kids. You love them, you do their laundry, make 10,000 meals for them. Then they leave home, just as they are becoming proper human beings. Natural and normal, right? Well, I think it stinks!

As teenagers they gradually weaned me of their presence by earning their driver's licences, and no longer needed my frequent chauffeuring services. Part-time jobs usurped the leisurely lying around and hanging about they had done in their early teens. The umbilical cord was almost severed.

By the time they were in grade 12, I could catch the occasional glimpse as one or the other flashed by, returning late from a babysitting job, or a Tim Horton's shift. A two-minute visit at breakfast was a rare treat before they tore off to school.

Slowly, slowly, they were acclimatizing me to their eventual permanent departure. I was aware of this, knowing it was right and inevitable, but I never really liked the idea.

I thought I was doing parenting right: I gave them responsibility and enough leeway to make their own decisions and their own mistakes. The feedback I've received would indicate they were socially acceptable, and they have made me proud many times.

They blew me away on September 1, 2002 by both leaving home the same day. Jenny relocated to new digs near the University of Victoria, and Mike to new Katimavic adventures in Prince George. I read them the Riot Act. I explained that this was not in our contract: two siblings were expressly forbidden to leave home on the same day.

64

They pointed out that there was a clause in said contract stating that if one of the children was born on the same day as the mother, the contract was null and void. Because Mike was born on my birthday, they had me. With a heavy heart, I shuffled boxes for Jen and arranged plane tickets for Mike.

For a week or two, I was accepting of our emptier house and our fuller milk cartons. After weeks of trying to remember to set four places instead of six, I realized that I wasn't as indifferent as I was making out to be.

Maybe what I was really scared of was the fact that they can live without me. Hmm. Luckily, we still have two boys at home. Surely they will never leave?

I miss you, Jenny and Mike.

      Love Mom,
      XOXOXO

Sibling Unrivalry

There has been much written in popular magazines about sibling rivalry and other frictions between sibs. The following tale is an example of the companionship and friendship that can exist between children in the same family.

I'll start this saga with a sweet little girl, nearly three years old, who dearly wanted a Cabbage Patch doll. Her father wasn't fond of the whole Cabbage Patch craze that had gripped the nation and was often heard referring to them as Cabbage Patch ripoffs.

The sweet girl's mother was pleased as, up until now, her daughter had shown no interest in dolls in general. Mom had a plan. She battled the crowd at a department store and was able to purchase a brown-haired moppet Cabbage Patch doll with the unlikely moniker of Gilda Irena. Each doll came with its own name documented on its "adoption" papers.

Several months passed before the expectant momma was to relinquish the dolly. The subsequent birth of the wee girl's sibling would be the impetus for the gift of Gilda.

On arrival home from the hospital, the baby brother, with a little help, presented his sister with her most sought-after desire. She was delirious with delight, shouting "Look, a Cabbage Patch rip-off!" The wonder, joy and exhilaration on her face was a marvelous sight. She was to connect her joy with Gilda to the arrival of her brother forever more.

That first meeting of the two-day-old baby and his three-year-old sister was to set the tone of their relationship from that day in 1984 to this very day.

What would have happened if her brother had given her a truck? We'll never know, but I will leave you with one final anecdote. Fast forward, and the then 17-year-old boy was

66

overheard in discussion with one of his friends, who was complaining about what a pain his older sister was. The doll giver responded, sounding rather puzzled, "I really like my sister. She's cool!" My heart swelled with pride. What better compliment could I, his mother, receive?

Our two youngest sons get along famously, too, except there's no Cabbage Patch doll involved.

(Big sister Jenny and Mike, 1985)

(Sweaters knit by their Granny, 1986)

Where is My Green Bowl?

Can you help me to find my green bowl? I'm sure I've taken it to a potluck or party with Japanese Coleslaw in it — or maybe Double Chocolate Bombe. It's the middle bowl of a set of three, and my favourite. It makes everything you put in it look tasty.

The last time I used it I remember thinking I should use one of my expendable receptacles. "Oh, no, I won't forget to take it home" I admonished myself. When will I learn?

This story isn't about lost kitchen vessels. It's about my memory. When I was younger, I often wondered why older people seemed to be obsessed with talking about their forgetfulness. I'm beginning to get a glimmer of the gradual slipperiness that memory presents.

Several years ago, in December, my partner remarked several times that he was worried about my mental state. The problem manifested itself as muddling up small details such as not turning off a stove burner or confusing the car-pooling schedule.

Miraculously, in January, I regained my previous mental acuity. Christmas stress and all the related tasks definitely had affected my mental sharpness.The next festive Christmas season served to confirm the reason for my temporary lapses.

This past Christmas I cut back on many of the less important, probably self-induced, activities and noticed fewer blanks in my memory bank. Message: Slow down and concentrate on the important objective of the season: family and friends. The rest is just window dressing.

While I was growing up in Union Bay, just south of Courtenay, B.C., we had a senior neighbour who wrote down everything in a notebook she carried with her. I thought it was a habit she had picked up while she was a newspaper reporter. I now realize it was her way of coping with a failing memory. Note to self: try to remember to buy a notebook.

Memory has such a funny way of choosing what it wants to retain. Why do I remember the details of the dress I wore to my first Grade 8 dance, but have no memory of the events of the dance itself? No, I wasn't imbibing anything back then.

I've tried taking Ginko Biloba for memory enhancement, but I forgot where I stored it. (Groan! Pathetic memory joke).

My most treasured memories, which I will never forget, involve the feel of my babies' heads, the joy of their sticky hugs and the wonder of watching them find their places in the world.

Remember, keep a watch for my green bowl!

Birth of a Bow Tie Maker

How does one go about becoming a bow tie maker? I certainly didn't grow up wanting to be one, although in Grade 3 I did write an essay (all six sentences) about wanting to be a factory worker — an unusual dream for an Air Force brat.

Sewing has been the background of my life, taking many side roads along the way, into different modalities and utilizing interesting fabrics. Although I am not artistic, I believe I am creative, with fabric being my favourite medium.

Having dabbled for a short time as a quilter, I decided I didn't have that certain magic eye that my sister Janine has — the ability to put many different colours and patterns together in a pleasing fashion. The ability to marry a variety of disparate materials in a homogeneous way has eluded me. Well, I can take a hint. The Universe has no plans for me to be a quilter.

My great friend Kathy Griffiths, Kathy of Gumboot Bakery fame (a long-time institution at the local Sunday farmers' market), disparages the whole quilting concept. Her thinking follows this train of thought: "You take a perfectly good lengths of fabric, cut them into small bits, then sew them back together again!" She makes a good argument, but I admire most quilting efforts — they have an otherworldly, immeasurable quality that is hard for me to quantify.

Although my quilting efforts were short-lived, I did manage to acquire a great stash of lovely textiles. What should I sew now?

On a whim, I made a bow tie and immediately, I mean IMMEDIATELY, fell in love with the sweet bow made from a small piece of floral-patterned material. Not having anyone in my circle to wear it. I started wearing it myself, and made a dozen more to match various outfits I had in my punk frump wardrobe.

That was 2011. As I had an Etsy shop[2] with a few crafted items, I decided to list in it a few of the excess bow ties that I was compulsively making. The first bow tie I sold, on November 12, 2011, had a nautical sailboat design. I was so pleased!

It occurred to me then that I could specialize in theme-based accessories. Superheroes were/are popular, so they were my next focus. Superman, Batman and Spiderman fabrics were quickly sourced and fabricated into smart and sought-after products.

My creative ability came handily to the fore, as I wanted to accentuate and center the character on each piece of fabric. It's called fussy cutting, and takes a lot of trial and error to technically succeed. It's basically designing: precisely cutting and stitching the figure equidistant on each side of the front of the bow tie.

Initially, I was happy to sell two or three of these ties each month. Six months after my first bow tie sale on Etsy, over the May long weekend, I had 17 sales of my Superman Comics bow tie. "Overwhelmed" would be a gross understatement of my joyous reaction to this unexpected and unexplained influx of orders!

I immediately called Jenny, my librarian daughter, who researched and found the cause of the deluge of orders. A famous blogger had written about this now-iconic (in my mind, anyway) shirt accessory, and 67 bloggers of note re-blogged his positive reaction to my product on Tumblr. This was a fantastic introduction for me to the wonder and power of social media.

This sequence of events set me on a life-altering route to the realization that I could, indeed, "live the dream" as a self-employed Maker.

Several years would pass before I resigned my 40-hour-a-week employment as a cashier (that I practised for 28 years at Save On Foods in the Saanich Plaza in Victoria, B.C.)

---

[2] Etsy is an e-commerce company.

At the time of this writing, my Etsy shop is still selling my bow ties, and I still love sewing them.

www.etsy.com/shop/sewfairycute

It looks like I am a factory worker now, but I also own the factory! The dream of an eight-year-old came true. Lucky me!

(A selction from the Specialty Collection)

(A selection from Brights Collection)

Am I Teacher or Student?

Have you ever met someone and had the feeling that they would change the course of your life? No? Me either.

My friend Xinghua (pronounced Shing Wha) didn't change my life trajectory, but he certainly helped me to expand my understanding of my comfortable lifestyle.

Our relationship began in 1997 when he answered an ad I had posted at the University of Victoria for a student to rent a room and share a rental house in the Gordon Head area. I was a single Mom with two young kids and needed someone to babysit several evenings a week while I worked. I figured a university pupil would be ideal.

Initially I was aghast at the thought of a male stranger caring for my kids, until I met him and realized that he'd be great for us all.

Xinghua moved in a few days later. He had been in Canada for only five days, having arrived from Beijing, China, to attend graduate classes in geophysics at UVic towards his PhD.

His personal mission was to live with a Canadian family and experience our Canadian way of life. Improving his English was also paramount to our new friend and housemate. Coaching him in our idiomatic English language was as enlightening to me as it was to him. Helping him to understand the whys and wherefores was ever so much fun. There were many times when he questioned some point of my mother tongue and I had no answer. More times than not, though, I could reply to his query, and that made this high school graduate feel smart.

Many things came under his scrutiny, giving me a fresh look at our everyday processes and motivations. The morning he came to live with us, we took him for a Springtime walk around the neighbourhood. He pointed to a man who happened to be mowing his lawn and mentioned to me "You have one of those machines in your basement". Surprised at his commenting on something as mundane as a lawn mower, I asked "Don't you have mowers for parks in Beijing?" He replied that the public use of the parks was so heavy that there was no need for mowing. Imagine: grass worn down to nubs by foot traffic.

Another day, about six months into our time together, while I was tidying up after dinner, I needed to rinse my hands and quickly plunged them into his sink of dishes. Much to my horror, his wash water was stone cold! "What are you doing?" I queried. "Washing my dishes" was his rejoinder. When I explained that he should be using hot water, he was perplexed. I elaborated on the comfort and health benefits of using at least warm water for dish cleansing. I came away from this exchange understanding how extravagant running hot water must be to someone who grew up without it. Wow! I felt spoiled and unappreciative of the privileged life I absolutely took for granted.

I ashamedly knew nothing of the China my friend grew up in and had left in order to come to our beautiful Province. I learned incredible facts about conditions he grew up in during his childhood. The most heartbreaking situation he revealed to me was that he had never wanted to be a geophysicist, as his interests lay in biomedics. He was chosen to study earthquakes and the like and had no recourse but to study this field right through to his PhD. Years and years with dedication but no passion.

I'll end this tale with my favourite story of our Chinese pal. He bought a lottery ticket on his second day in Canada and won $2,000. How could he not believe the streets were paved with gold in his new home, Canada? The money lasted him a long time. I thought I was a thrifty person, but he was a shining beacon of careful money managing.

Many times, during our year and a half together, he inadvertently showed me how wasteful our culture was and how much we took for granted, wealth wise, health-wise and mentally.

Xinghua — my teacher, my friend.

(Xinghua, the author and husband Pete, 1989)

Going Home

My mother, my daughter and I were finally winging our way towards Eastern Canada, on a farewell tour for my Mom, who suffered from terminal pancreatic cancer. She was born and raised on Prince Edward Island, the second of six children. North Rustico, a small lobster fishing village, was our specific destination.

I spent eight years as a child in Summerside, where my Air Force Dad was stationed. A thirty-minute drive away from North Rustico, we spent many lovely visits with grandparents, aunts, uncles and innumerable cousins. Mom was going home, but I felt I was, too.

We were sad that our trip was going to be a time of goodbyes for my mother, but planned it around my cousin's wedding. That meant all the far-flung relatives from Montreal and Toronto would be there, too, to celebrate a happier occasion than our sad objective.

We flew to Montreal, where we rented a car and toured through Quebec, admiring the different scenery and all the church spires.

My rusty high school French turned out to be inadequate when dealing with a French speaking RCMP officer who stopped us (me) for speeding just inside the New Brunswick border. Because we had Quebec plates on our rented car, he initiated our conversation with "Bonjour". "Bonjour" I responded. "Oh, you speak English" he replied. He could tell from that one word that my French-Acadian heritage had failed me.

After some discussion on his car phone, he let me off with a warning. I think my B.C. driver's licence and my rented Quebec plates in his New Brunswick jurisdiction would have been too much paperwork for him. I woke up on the right side of the bed that day.

Chastened, we made our way more slowly across that amazing Confederation bridge to P.E.I. It's an exceptional engineering feat that gives the Island folk better and more consistent access to Canada's mainland.

Immediately on our arrival, cousins, aunts, uncles and even more cousins and second cousins drew us into a hectic round of visiting, reminiscing, and much hugging and kissing. The Montreal contingent's manner of kissing both cheeks delighted me.

The wedding was resplendent with a beaming bride, gallant groom, a thunder and lighting rain deluge, a two-hour power outage, and much dancing through it all.

The next day we visited the setting of my all-time favourite book, Green Gables, in Cavendish. I wish we hadn't. Anne wasn't home that day.

We also toured Slemon Park, which was the living quarters, the PMQs, where I spent my formative years. I was reluctant to visit, as I thought things would have changed drastically. They hadn't, so I was glad we took that detour.

We ate lobsters. Delicious. You haven't lived until you have experienced a North Rustico lobster dinner. Do it, please.

Our visit came to an end. It was time to do what we had come to accomplish. A goodly selection of our relations met us on the beach on which we had spent so much time all through the 1960s. It was late afternoon, with a slight breeze blowing.

Somberly we held hands, facing the water. I took out the container we had so lovingly transported to Mom's homeland. Choking out a short goodbye, I shook out my beloved mother's ashes and wished her safe travels. Her ashes swirled around us, bidding us a final farewell before disappearing into the Gulf of St. Lawrence.

Mary Pauline Welch was home.

Beakball — A New Spectator Sport

I invented a new spectator sport today. Actually, our neighbour's poultry developed it, but I immediately saw its possibilities. I am thinking we should call it Beakball.

This is what I saw. I threw a good-sized heel of French bread to the waiting fowl. They instantly scrambled into action. The nearest biddy grabbed the hunk of bread with her beak (hence Beakball) and went tearing down the field with 14 other hens in hot pursuit. She then flicked her head and passed the beakball to the nearest hen.

At first I assumed that the hen she had passed it to was on her team, as they all had the same brown-feathered look to them. But no, the supposed teammate made a mad dash in the opposite direction! She was only pretending to be on the same team. She had run only about a metre before a third biddy stole the beakball and tore off on a third trajectory. I think it was the third hen. Maybe it was the first hen? I am not too sure.

After many more "passes" and "steals" the beakball disappeared. No hard feelings, though. They all seemed quite happy with the game's outcome, even though there were several loud skirmishes during the game.

A big selling point for Beakball is the short amount of time it takes to play. Three minutes, maybe. Five for a really big chunk of bread.

I wonder if our neighbour would mind if I sewed up some little bibs to help keep track of the teams as they play?

Deception, Manipulation and Bribery

This title might bring images to mind of the sort we often have come to associate with politics. I don't dwell on political dealings of any sort, so I will spare you any inept efforts on my part to wax eloquent on that topic. Rather, I am going to blather on about something I have had much experience with: Motherhood. Four times. Best times ever.

At this juncture, I must make it quite clear that the following are my experience and my theories, and not those of any other person, either real or imagined, living or dead. And these aren't recommendations, either — just my mothering journey written down here.

In my early twenties I had a clear idea about the sort of parent I was going to be. The following discourse does not reflect my previously imagined model at all. What follows is a record of a mom of a daughter and three sons, all learning how to exist in a family setting.

My kiddos were good children, in my unbiased opinion, but our trip together involved DECEPTION. This is not a trait I ever thought I would aspire to, but I found myself in conversations with mamas of other youngsters, advising them to practice deception, too! I, of course, didn't call it that, I called it "getting cooperation" from one's offspring.

I'll give you several examples. You have decided to provide the maximum amount of nutrition with a minimum amount of power struggle. Get out your blender. My kids have ingested more blended vegetables in their spaghetti sauce and chili con carne than they will ever know. Carrots' colour melds wonderfully with the red tomato sauce. Blended tofu figured often in my soups, sauces and desserts. Home-made fish sticks were called chicken strips, and were enjoyed by my table mates more than if they were called by the correct name. Get my drift?

If you try these tricks, don't succumb to smugly informing your charges of your subterfuge. All you will accomplish is to cause endless speculation and balking at every dish you present to them for the next ten years.

A laundry switcheroo I frequently employed solved a situation of perception my daughter had with the oversized sweatshirts she favoured wearing in her teens. These garments, with no apparent soiling, worn once over a t-shirt, would appear in the laundry basket. No amount of explaining the cost and effort of washing a completely clean top made any impact. I quickly formulated this coping mechanism to save both our sanities. I would fluff it in the dryer for three minutes, fold it up and pass it off as a freshly laundered garment. I didn't and don't condone lying, but I never CLAIMED I had washed the sweatshirts and she never asked.

MANIPULATION was my second talent of which I am not proud. This tale involves my 13-year-old son and a gorgeous Spring Sunday morning. The phone rang and it was Mike, who had spent the night at a friend's house. He wanted a ride home.

The distance was about a kilometer, I was busy gardening, and there was no reason he couldn't walk home. "Please walk home" I politely commanded. "No" my son intoned. "Someone might see my sleeping bag" he pleaded. Much back and forth ensued. A manipulation strategy came to my mind. "OK. We'll be up to get you."

I went into the house and put on my most kid-embarrassing outfit, a hot pink jogging suit. I proceeded to walk up to Mike's friend's house, with Rudy, Mike's five-year-old brother, in tow. When Mike came out through the door, he asked smugly, "Where is the car?" I replied "The car? I didn't say I would drive you home."

A chagrined Mike walked home with us, none too pleased. But to his credit, he grasped my point without whining. He knew a smooth Mom manipulation when he saw it.

BRIBERY is my least favourite parenting leverage. Every other trick failed to get youngest son Rudy to eat many of my dinner selections. Quiet explanations, threats, pleading — all were of no effect, but offer dessert as an enticement and his plate was spotless, almost instantly!

The after-meal treat didn't have to be fancy or particularly sweet. Fruit salad, apple crisp or banana tofu pudding was consumed with gusto. You can't argue with the results, and the rest of the family benefited, too.

The second bribery example involved Jenny, our first born. When she was little, I was very very strict about exposing her to sugar and, as a consequence, she consumed virtually none. When it came time for toilet training, she wasn't much impressed with the cute little panties or the possibility of freeing her cute tush from the bondage of diapers.

With a heavy heart, I bought a box of Smarties and began the shortest toilet training session ever recorded. Maybe I am exaggerating, just a bit, but, two Smarties were offered for positive potty action, and BOOM! Done and dusted. That girl responded so quickly to this method that I thought about patenting it. After emptying most of the Smarties out of the box, away from her view, I used up the last few candies over the next couple of days, while cementing the potty routine into her life. As she saw the box becoming empty, and not understanding that the store had a million Smartie containers, after the last two candies were offered as potty payment, she understood, as she saw the empty cardboard container, that all the sweets were gone. Ta da!

How did I veer so far from the starry-eyed standards I held before having all my lovely kids? Perhaps having at least one child under six years old for 16 years contributed to my use of questionable coping mechanisms.

Maybe motherhood is one long lesson in coping. I loved the lesson and those I learned it from.

Fancy Nancy and Robert Munsch Save the Day

This story begins one bright Springtime morning on my Granny Nanny day, with no indication anything untoward was about to happen. My granddaughter, Mairi, six years old at the time, was in my charge and being dropped off at her school for the start of her day. I was accompanied by Mairi's little sister, Madeline, three years old, and we were planning to do our grocery shopping after this drop-off.

I buckled the pixie Madeline into her car seat and placed several picture books into her lap for the short drive to our shopping destination. As I was shutting her door I became aware of the locks on all the doors clicking into the locked position. As I had just thrown my keys on the front seat, the locking mechanism must have been universally activated. The school parking lot suddenly seemed forbidding, as the reality of my conundrum hit me.

For all intents and purposes, the car was now my youngest granddaughter's prison. I immediately went into panic mode. What were my options? Call BCAA? No, that could take too long. My husband was working out of town, so he wasn't able to help me out of this terrible pickle. Calling our neighbours was the obvious solution.

My overriding concern was keeping my diminutive passenger calm. I took out my cell phone and forgot how to operate it. I was losing my grip on my sanity, but had to pull myself out of my hysteria. My muscle memory finally kicked in and I punched in the Corwins' number, praying that someone was home. The four adults living next door to us had varied working schedules and I was hoping that one of them might be passing near our location and could deliver our spare car keys.

My friend Tracy answered and quickly deduced I was in full hysteria mode and needed her help. She rapidly located our extra house key, hidden under our compost bin, and let herself into the house to obtain the spare vehicle key. She then dragged her daughter Madeleine (same name as my lovely, but different spelling) out of bed to drive. (Tracy was unable to drive due to painkillers in her system, because she had had the end of her finger bitten off the night before by a dog.)

I hung up after learning that the rescue party was on its way to restore my fragile hold on sanity and turned my attention to hoping my lovely engrossed preschooler remained preoccupied.

The sun was shining and I now began to worry that the backseat munchkin might be in danger of overheating. I splayed my torso across the back window, blocking out the sunbeams' trajectory, and tried not to look like a bloated, frumpy starfish. Miss M was so engrossed in her *Fancy Nancy* book that she took no notice of her eccentric Granny doing sprawling poses across her side window.

She never did express any interest in what I was doing and why there was a delay in our departure from the school parking lot. When she tired of her first choice of book, I shouted through the window that she should check out the Robert Munsch book.

Twelve long, but really very short, minutes passed before Tracy and her groggy driver skidded to a stop beside us, threw us the key, and tore away, confident in the knowledge they had earned the four plates of fudge I would soon deliver to their door as payment for the swift delivery of the sanity-saving car key.

Madeline was never the wiser about her enforced confinement, and my few remaining brown hairs are now grey. I'll have to find a new hiding place for our spare key, because now you all know where our hiding place is.

Wanted: Ruminator

If I saw a newspaper advertisement looking for a ruminator, this is the application I would submit for the job, assuming they wanted a frivolous ruminator, of course:

I am applying for your company's position as ruminator, as my friends will attest that I am well suited to ruminations of all manner of silliness. Please note examples as follows:

1. I have been doing several ongoing informal surveys over the last ten years and here are my results:

a) 93% of liver lovers co-habitat with non-lovers of liver.

b) The general population is split evenly into two camps: those who wear underwear to bed and those who don't. This is from a random sample from four participants. Math isn't my best subject, but I believe that is a 50/50 split.

c) People either have canker sores or cold sores — Rarely both, and rarely neither. I forgot my notebook the day I did this survey, so you'll have to take my word on this one. (Echinacea tincture dabbed on a canker at its first tingle will be miraculous in stopping its progression. I'm a canker sufferer myself.)

2. Conspiracy theories I suspect:

a) Colds are perpetrated by cold remedy companies. Perhaps the companies partner with tissue manufacturers who impregnate the tissues with viruses to create need for their products.

b) Grass was invented by lawn mower corporations to prevent us resting and relaxing on the weekends.

c) We have put men on the moon and beyond. Why can't scientists make it rain from midnight to 6:00 a.m.?

3. Financial speculations:

   a) I'll be richer by NOT buying lottery tickets than by purchasing them.

   b) It would be tragic if I suddenly became wealthy. I've had so much experience being poor, it would be a shame to waste all the thrifty expertise I have gathered.

   c) I wish that I smoked, so I could quit and have a lot of extra money.

This concludes my ruminations for the moment. I have many more, should you want more of my ruminations, speculations or theories.

What do you think? Should I keep my day job?

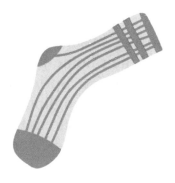

The Fudge Fairy

There was once a girl, an ordinary teenage girl, who dreamed of designing and making fabric. As she became older, she sadly realized that she had no artistic talent. The dream was left behind as she grew up, took an ordinary job, married, and raised extraordinarily wonderful children.

Time passed. The woman fostered a creative tendency coupled with an entrepreneurial streak that manifested itself in a variety of different guises. A sewing pattern for a cloth diaper kept her busy until the cloth diaper craze pooped out. Her Wee Washables were all washed up.

The next enterprise involved her octopus-diving husband and the smoked octopus they produced and marketed. A great and tasty product that the bulk of the public was not ready for. The concept was just too "outside the box".

Undaunted, she and her husband embarked on running a shrub nursery. They sold their home-grown shrubbery from the end of their driveway. The first Spring brought a number of gardeners to purchase from the fledgling selection of bushes. As the Spring wore on, it became apparent that the nursery needed an alternative draw to entice would-be consumers to continue to check for the latest nursery stock as it matured and appeared on the stand.

The creative, but not artistic, woman was also a maker of tasty fudge, so that is what she chose to offer to augment the plant selection. Chocolate and butterscotch were the first two flavours on offer. Soon peanut butter, coffee mocha and chocolate mint fudge were added to the sweet roster.

The Fudge Lady soon realized that the general public enjoyed her fudge from the farm stand and so she spent more time in the kitchen and less time working in the shrubbery.

As the Summer wore on, the number of flavours grew. Maple walnut, chocolate orange, root beer and coconut creme came into being. The shapes and sizes of the confectionery evolved. Gift packaging was concocted and many samples were distributed.

Now The Fudge Lady came to realize that the fudge business was what she was born for. Her calling. Her creative outlet. Twenty flavours, then 25. It was the day that bubble gum fudge was invented that she realized she had the fudge touch.

This story culminated at the 1999 Metchosin Day, her local fall fair event. The Fudge Lady was making her first public appearance. The sales were brisk. Rudy, her eight-year-old son, materialized at her side with a gift he and his 11-year-old brother, Max, had designed at the plastic button booth. The candy maker read the button, paused, and became the persona the boys had portrayed on the button. An awesome stick figure was shown with a big smile, and in her hand she held a magic wand. The Fudge Fairy was born.

The children of the Fudge Fairy were supportive, to a point. None of them would wear buttons claiming "My Mom's the Fudge Fairy" or paste bumper stickers on their cars saying "The Fudge Fairy Lives!". But they sure volunteered to scrape the warm fudge left after a batch was poured! Lucky kids.

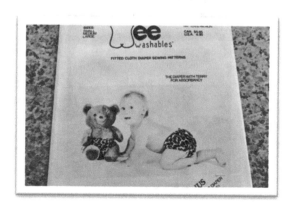

(Max on cover of the author's diaper sewing pattern)

My Family Suffers From T.H.S.

(Note to readers: I chose not to update this story from its originally published form in the 2002 Metchosin Muse. Some things shouldn't be messed with. But it was edited, so yes — it was messed with.)

My family suffers from T.H.S. We haven't always had it. This condition occurred gradually over the last 13 years and is now at a critical level.

For those of you who live in a large house, this will be an unfamiliar condition. T.H.S. stands for "Tiny House Syndrome" and for us it was the result of the culmination of many factors, sometimes happening simultaneously:

- Size of house (tiny)
- Number of family members (six)
- Physical size of occupants (small to large and everything in between)
- Noisiness of those inhabiting the residence (one of them really rowdy)
- Organizational ability of the cook (well, a definite fail here)
-

When we moved into our teeny abode we had two small children, rather quiet by nature, and an inactive, layabout cat, in a three-bedroom, one-bathroom house. As time rambled on, as it is wont to do, we added two more children (the rowdy one appeared last) and exchanged our sedentary cat for an acrobatic Siamese-cross kitty.

We added an addition to the house to try to stem the effects of the voraciousness of the T.H.S. You know, as I am explaining this to you, I think we have graduated from T.H.S. to the rarer

M.H.M.T.R.S. (Medium House Many Tiny Rooms Syndrome). We now have five small bedrooms, a miniature doll-sized computer room, a little sewing room (OK, it's an enlarged hallway), a minuscule pantry, two bathrooms (thank Heavens), a middle-sized kitchen (another enlarged hallway) and an infinitesimally petite dining room/living room.

All these rooms are miniature and the layout is like no other you have ever seen. I liken it to a rabbit warren.

Having a peculiar, tiny-roomed house has its challenges. Of that I can attest, as can my household roomies. Storage of items not used daily can be a struggle. Having a full family turkey dinner takes three days of planning — and that's just for the seating arrangements!

Our organizational skills have been honed over the years. Some of our furniture does double duty. A large upholstered trunk, rescued from the side of the road, serves as seating for three on one side of the kitchen/dining table. The commodious trunk interior serves as storage for seasonal clothing.

Loft beds built into two of the bedrooms are a design choice that affords more floor space for toy-playing activity. OK, probably a lot of detritus as well, toys and castoff clothes, I suspect. Alright, already! I don't suspect, I know there are random wardrobe items. I get behind in the laundry sometimes, Sheesh!

My friends know I am always commenting about our residence and its lack of space, but I love a challenge, and this one's a dilly!

And if this is the worst thing that's ever happened to our kids, they'll be doing alright.

(Original house.)

(Our house as it is now.)

Grey is My Disguise

Who is that old woman sleeping beside my husband? He is snuggled up against her ample back rather intimately. Her long grey hair is fanned out rather messily over the familiar burgundy pillowcase.

As I scan her facial features, recognition dawns on me. That wrinkly face is mine! What happened to the young wife and mother who, seemingly months ago, inhabited that chubby, unyoung body? I guess I am newly old.

This aging situation is a blessing and a curse. I am grateful to have lived long enough to become aged, but so surprised that it happened as quickly as it has. This is a reality most people of senior years grapple with.

I have learned a new word while writing this article, and it so well describes this process. Senescent, or biological, aging, is the gradual deterioration of functional characteristics.

Oh, boy! What fun!

As an optimistic person, I am concentrating on the positive aspects of growing older — you know, all the good things that come with Seniordom: the 10% discount at the Salvation Army, the old age pension, no more wolf whistles. What else? I am digging deep here.

OK. Let's talk adaptations. I have learned that my body can't hula hoop like it used to, as I found out while showing my granddaughter how I can't hula like I used to. My running gait has turned into plodding pace. My svelte silhouette has blossomed into a short, round profile.

This may sound rather negative, but I am trying to be realistic here. My positive realizations include the concept that I finally understand that I can be who I've always wanted to be: a gregarious, amicable, sociable individual who isn't concerned anymore about what people think of her.

Somehow my grey hair has turned into my superpower. I don't have to prove my worth anymore. I can glide into my dotage confident that I have accomplished much by being a loving mum to our four kids and wife to the old man who sleeps beside me every night.

Sweet dreams, old lady!

"I hate housework. You make the beds, you wash the dishes and six months later you have to start all over again." – Joan Rivers

Herding Cats

After three years of a very sheltered Covid existence, I was off to Kingston, Ontario to visit our son Rudy and his wife, Maya. Two days prior to my departure, my daughter, Jen, reminded me to print out my boarding pass. Right. Good idea.

As she is my life organizational assistant, I rely on Jenny, probably too much, to keep my life uncomplicated. Well, as simple as she has the power to orchestrate, from eight kilometres away. I don't know why I mention the distance, because these days, with so many methods to communicate, any distance isn't a barrier to life helpmates. She even has an app on her phone that tells her at what location I can be found at any time. Wow!

Some people might find this level of surveillance to be creepy. Not me. I feel I have a remote guardian angel hovering just out of sight. Many might resent the type of involvement my oldest child has with me. I don't. While I am rather scatterbrained and slightly lazy, she valiantly and mostly successfully keeps my life on track.

Where does my husband fit into this scenario? Does he have input into my daily routines? He does, but his life hints and tips don't always jibe with my vibe. Jen has known me all her life, but Pete's been involved only for the last 35 years. His strength is the big picture and the long game consequences.

Please don't worry that I monopolize all her time and keep her from her obligations to her full-time librarian job, two daughters and our son-in-law, Iain. Some people are born co-coordinators, able to juggle multiple project balls in unison. Jen aced the Life 101 course while taking her master's degree, and I am so proud of all she has accomplished.

She can herd cats, too.

(Jenny and the author)

Face Plant

My official introduction to volunteerism was undertaken with much trepidation. I was "voluntold" into a secretarial position as a director for a local arts organization. I was happy to explore new experiences in my dotage, but knew the secretary opportunity was not going to be a good fit. As my friends and family will attest: my organizational skills are incredibly underdeveloped.

Betty, the dedicated and enthusiastic director who recruited me, was quite certain that I would soon catch on with help from Gail, the secretary-treasurer. Gail was retaining the treasurer position, but was very ready and willing to help me settle into this new challenge.

On the surface, this position looked easy and the time commitment really was a once-a-month board meeting, where I was to take the minutes. Easy peasy. My Grade nine shorthand capability would have come in handy, had I been able to recall any of it. Gail suggested I type the minutes directly into my laptop. Ah, no. My rocky relationship with computers is legendary. Maybe I should write a story about that. No. No. No. I had too many horrific instances of the afflictions the computer has rained down on me over the years. I could not subject myself to those past traumas again.

Using my sketchy penmanship, I proceeded with the apparently defunct cursive language with which I have had a much happier relationship. For six board meetings, I scribbled furiously to note down all the possible words I could scribe. As I later realized, a good recorder can make concise decisions quickly as to what is relevant to record for posterity. My minutes looked more like novelettes than precise condensations of the proceedings. As I was a neophyte board member, I was trying to absorb the inner workings and nuances of this worthy, local art-promoting group of committed volunteers.

Looking back at the minutes I recorded, I recognized I had developed a different format for the minutes for each month. As I had tried to capture all comments and as I am a two fingered typist, the result took me ages to complete. Sometimes I was just distributing the previous month's minutes as we sat down for the next month's board meeting.

During the first half-year I was included in this lovely band of art enthusiasts, I enjoyed our camaraderie. The reality of my hinky recording ability caught up with me just before our seventh board meeting. Our president, Chris, asked to have a private word before the meeting convened. As I settled into my seat at our office table, he gently inquired if I would mind ceding the secretary position back to Gail. I doubt that he anticipated my shouted reply, "Are you kidding me? I would LOVE to!" He looked rather taken aback at my lusty reply. I received the impression that he may have expected me to cry. I am, after all, a self-professed thin-skinned individual.

I am now a happy volunteer who prefers to be given specific tasks with precise instructions. I appreciated the opportunity to fall so spectacularly on my face.

(In the BCCA office: Gail Nash on left, the author in centre and Betty Hildreth on right.)

Necessary Holidays

Which do you like better: packing to go on holiday, or packing to go home? Me? Hmm. Well, I love the delicious anticipation of speculating how many novels I'll read or what tasty snacks we might indulge in. I enjoy the challenge of packing just the right amount of clothing to avoid doing laundry while away.

I should explain. For years we rented a cabin on Denman Island, a four-hour journey from our cozy home. This rustic rental cottage, a converted logging bunkhouse, featured a fully stocked kitchen. The rustic setting included an outhouse as the "ick" factor in an otherwise idyllic setting.

The four bedrooms were decked out with beds sporting mattresses bought shortly after Sir John A. MacDonald became our first Prime Minister in 1867. A bit of hyperbole, but not far from reality.

The location on 10 acres of private beachfront more than compensated for the lumpy beds and lack of flush toilets. Glorious sunsets didn't hurt, either.

There was nowhere to spend money and nothing to do except relax and spend time on the beach. No television, telephones or computers.

Sounds ideal, right? Yes, I really enjoyed my first five or six days there, but even though all my family was there with me, I still missed home. One year we decided to rent our island retreat for two weeks and I just about went berserk. Did I miss my bed, my routine or my sewing machine? Who knows for sure? As the saying goes "Home is best".

Nothing makes my heart soar more than to be on our way home after our time away. One mile to go, two blocks to go, THERE'S OUR DRIVEWAY. Our funny house, our antisocial cat, all the dirty laundry to deal with. Heaven! My own bed!

The other type of holiday I tend to enjoy is the visit-your-friends-and-family type of vacation. This is enjoyable on several levels. Foremost, lots of talking and catching up on each others' lives. A borrowed phrase comes to mind: "Gossip — the close analysis of interpersonal relationships."

It is the close-up look at the way other people live that piques my interest. After visiting friends who have a depressed teen who suffers week-long migraines, I can be thankful for happy and healthy children. Spending time with another friend who has a terminally ill and dependent mother opens my eyes to the virtue of hale and hearty relatives. A third friend, with a spouse who suffers from a tragic autoimmune disease, helps me appreciate my spouse's ability to do just about everything!

In summary: vacations were invented to make us appreciate real life. And what's better than living in this fantastic community with all the terrific people that live here? Lucky and grateful us.

(Left to right: Michael, Rudy, Peter, Max, the author, Mairi and Madeline, with Jenny and Iain in the rear.)

Shhh. Silence.

I never thought much about silence before. Never had much chance to experience it before. Being the oldest of five children, then having four kids of my own, silence just hasn't ever been an issue.

I've never missed it, or wanted it, or needed it. Couldn't actually see the point of it, really.

Then, in my late forties, silence was suddenly thrust upon me. My car radio broke at an inconvenient time, when I didn't have the time or money to have it fixed.

At first I fiddled with the knobs and buttons, trying to make the radio to put forth sound. As the car was a recent acquisition, I thought I wasn't finessing the radio hardware correctly.

Halfway to work I realized I wasn't getting my CBC fix that day. That was to be Day One of my silence experiment.

Day Two was spent driving along, knowing the radio wasn't working, but every five minutes or so automatically trying to turn up the volume. I was distinctly uncomfortable with the noise vacuum. I busied myself by mentally composing my shopping list.

By Day Three, I was REALLY missing noise. I was realizing how unaccustomed I was to my imposed silence and decided to study this phenomenon. Silence: a new frontier — for me, anyway.

What, really, was silence good for? Well, I discovered I can think more clearly with the radio off. I always have been able to block noise out, to think, or sleep, or study. Silence certainly takes the effort out of these processes.

Quiet can be more than the absence of noise. Silence can be restorative, meditative, and a pleasure.

After two weeks of one-hour-a-day enforced quietude, I had my radio repaired. I am now making a concerted effort to decide if I want the radio on for information or entertainment, or if it's just going to be background chatter. I learned that I can keep myself company, and I can be quite entertaining, given half a chance.

Silence and me. Friends at last.

"We come from dust and return to dust. That's why I don't dust. It could be someone I know."
- Unknown

Economic Supply and Demand

This isn't a dissertation on Federal economics. This is an explanation of how money fits into my life. Or, rather, flows through my wallet.

One Friday morning, a friend paid me the $400 they owed me. An hour later, on the way to the dentist, the mail revealed an unexpected income tax refund adjustment cheque of $342.20. At this juncture I was $742.20 to the good. I felt giddy thinking I might splurge on a quilting magazine and a new cookie sheet.

You know what's coming next, don't you?

A few minutes later, the dentist, on examining an errant molar, proclaimed I needed a $750 crown. My financial balance at this point was $7.80 in the red. Oh, well, my birthday was coming up. Maybe I'd get my cookie sheet and magazine then.

Another example of how the economic cosmos looks after me goes as follows: one day I had an important large cheque in my purse, with which I was to cover pending withdrawals. I had started my grocery cashiering shift at 8:30 a.m. and was to bank this important amount at my 12:30 lunch time.

At 11:30 a.m. my Uncle Harold, who lived near my place of employment, approached my workstation with a piece of paper in his hand. It was my cheque which, unbeknownst to me, had fallen out of my purse, just outside my car.

He had found it in the busy parking lot three hours after I had lost it. Looking at whom the cheque was made out to, recognizing my name, and knowing where I worked, my uncle had saved my financial bacon.

I am often heard to say, "All I want is my income to equal my expenses". This is pretty much what happens. We live fairly simply and we are happy.

This is my wish for you: that you live happily within your means and that you mean your happiness.

Can I Kick Organized Chaos?

In retrospect, my housekeeping technique of organized chaos harkens back to my childhood. Being a good Brownie and Girl Guide entailed "Being Prepared". This, to my detriment, was taken too literally.

As a "good" wife and mother, I have vowed to never be without any possible medicine, tool, foodstuff, gizmo or craft supply my family or friends might request. Heaven forbid someone needs saffron, googlie eyes, sequined shoes or a cold-mist humidifier and I cannot supply them. Somehow, my identity as a good person is tied up with my ability as a supplier.

My supply storage and retrieval process started going off the tracks about the time our fourth child was born. (My family would probably put this date about ten years earlier.) Part of my belief system involved having ten of certain items, whereas most people would have one or two. Scissors, rulers, vases, boots, bread pans, coats, umbrellas and water bottles were among my multiples collection. If you had lots of something, it increased your chance of finding one of these items when you needed it. Wrong!

My great friend and neighbour, Cathy Watson, inadvertently illuminated how misleading this thought process was. On entering her mudroom one day, I commented about how tidy it was and asked where she stored all their other shoes and boots, as I observed only one pair of each for each member of their family. Imagine my astonishment to learn that what I saw in front of me was all they needed.

Such an "aha" moment ensued that the effects are still reverberating in my stuff-stuffed life.

Now my brain synapses were flickering and the real work was to begin. My natural inclination was to look for books and courses to help me mitigate my problem. The Feng Shui *Clear*

Your Clutter course seemed to fit the bill. Yes. After the two-hour program, I was to take photos of treasures I did not want anymore, break some emotional ties with sentimental mementos and invest in a box of green garbage bags to haul away my junk. Piece of cake, right?

Hold on. I couldn't throw away everything, could I? Once in a while someone might need an umbrella, glue, or a recipe book, right? But which of the 150 recipe books should I keep? What if I threw out the wrong book?

It wasn't going to be that easy, after all. I had to sort through and make value judgments on all sorts of mundane knick-knacks and sentimental collections of treasured mementos.

Well, time to close this parable. I would like to say my house is now a picture of organizational bliss, but I would be lying. The best I can report at this time is that I have stopped frequenting thrift stores, where a lot of my duplicates and triplicates originated. And I have donated six garbage bags full of treasures and clothing BACK to them.

Am I cured? Not really. But at least I know how I got here. And that's half the battle, don'tcha think?

Ahhh!

This dissertation is about the Ahhh! moments in life. I have realized how many of them there are in my life. Ahhh occasions are different for everyone. Here are a few of mine.

I grew up in Prince Edward Island, and my earliest memories are connected to ice skating. Every winter my Dad made us an ice rink in our front yard, which provided the neighbourhood with a fabulous activity centre for five or six months of the year. After two hours of frenzied ice tag and crack the whip, that moment of releasing my feet from the confines of my skates was pure bliss! Can you feel it? Ahhh!

In the summer we lived at the beach and spent many hours frolicking in the water at the sandy beach in North Rustico, with many fun cousins. Slipping into our dry clothes after toweling off elicited sighs of comfort. Ahhh! Cozy!

As an adult, I have come to cherish and luxuriate in these times when they occur. My most frequent occurrence of this delicious feeling is the first ten or twenty seconds after I hit my bed at night. Stretching out — becoming one with the mattress — heavenly.

My next example is the yearly one many of you will be familiar with. Christmas. I love everything about this festive time, and it provides the biggest Ahhh of the year. It's really more like two or three days worth of "thank goodness it's over" — at least for another year. The tree is down, ornaments are nested away in the garage and the Christmas treats are nearly all devoured. It's all over but the bill paying.

In conclusion, it is your conclusion. Say Ahhh! Then relax and reflect on the peace and comfort your Ahhh moment brings you.

Until next time — Ahhh!

The Best Gifts

How many times have you heard the phrase "The best gifts can't be bought"? Health, love, and happiness come to mind. These are precious intangibles that sometimes are not appreciated until they are gone.

The mohair sweater and latest computer are nice gifts, but I will put them against the best presents I have ever received — Friendship and Empathy. I have been given these offerings many different times, but what follows are the best examples of both. Friendship was given by one of my dearest friends and empathy by a virtual stranger.

Many years ago I miscarried my fourth planned baby due to a twisted cyst on my ovary. I had the misfortune to suffer postpartum depression afterwards. I was only six weeks into the pregnancy, but was taking the loss very hard. The general consensus was that I was "just pregnant" and I had three other children (snap out of it was how I took those comments).

In retrospect, my family knew there had been a real possibility I would have bled to death had I not called my best friend, Kathy Cameron, to watch Max for me. Here is where the gift of Friendship kicks in.

I was having sharp abdominal pains and had made a doctor's appointment for the afternoon. Gas pains? I had never had gas pains before, but my mind diverted my attention away from the negative possibilities.

When Kathy answered the phone, she did not recognize my voice, even though we spoke every day. My distress-masked voice alerted her to bring her paramedic husband, Brad, when she came to pick up Max. The fact that I could not answer the door, and my plummeting blood pressure, were all Brad needed to alert the ambulance service, who whisked me to the emergency department.

The necessary emergency surgery saved my life, which resulted in the loss of my tiny embryo.

I am here today because of Kathy's friendship and will always be grateful for her instinct that day. And Brad's medical expertise, of course.

The empathy part of this same story occurred a month after that crisis. I was in the middle of my depression, and although my family was supportive, I felt isolated and alone in my grieving.

There was a knock on the door and a lady I barely knew thrust an envelope into my hand. She had heard of my woe, and although she did not know me, she was moved to write a most empathetic letter. It was all there, the emotions I was feeling, the depression I was dealing with. Her situation had been very similar to mine and the comradeship contained in that letter to a stranger was a tremendous comfort to me.

What a wonderful gesture from one mother to another. Thank-you Kathe. Same name, different spelling. I have written previously about my "Kathy collection", and now you know why I value them. They are, to a person, generous, kind and loyal.

The gifts of love and kindness are inexpensive but priceless. Give them often.

Housework Avoidance

As a girl raised in the 1960s, you might think I picked up many of the prevalent housekeeping trends popular back then. I'll leave you to decide the truth. As the oldest of five children, it was often the case that this birth order position would necessitate my participation in household chores. Let's examine the reality.

My Dad, David Welch, was in the Royal Canadian Air Force. Before I was born, my mother was enlisted, too. Actually, I am fond of saying I am a result of parachute packing. My parents met in 1953 as they both worked in the Safety Systems Section. Mom, Pauline Gauthier, had run away from her home in P.E.I. at the age of 16 and ended up in Centrailia, Ontario, where the old "opposites attract" mechanism worked its magic.

Back to the subject at hand. Mom was a stay-at-home mama of five kids. She was an avowed introvert and preferred no distractions while doing her housework. She would often put on a 33 LP of marching band music, because she said it helped her to do her work more quickly.

My housekeeping chore was riding herd on my four siblings while Mom cleaned, laundered and polished. Because our P.M.Q. (Permanent Married Quarters) was of rather austere décor, and we couldn't afford a lot of "stuff", her household upkeep was more simplistic than mine is today. While I was aware of her cleaning techniques, I didn't develop any muscle-memory memories from actual experience.

But, you might think, there are so many time-saving appliances now that they didn't have in the 60s. Yes, Mom used a wringer washer and hung the clothes on the clothesline, and used a floor polisher to wax our wooden floors. And yes, I have a dishwasher and an automatic clothes washer and dryer. So what's the point? Aha! You are starting to get it!

What IS the point? Wow. I, myself, am confused,. I think I have painted myself into a corner. Let me try again.

A different perspective. Everyone has different comfort levels regarding their cleanliness quotient. Early on in my first foray into sharing an apartment with two roommates, we hadn't developed a plan for the division of apartment cleaning duties.

One day I noticed our tiny white-tiled kitchen floor was filthy. Note the word noticed. I took it upon myself to wash it. Halfway through the task I stood back and admired my handiwork. Wow, such a difference! Some folks might have had that experience and been converted to the "Have an Amazingly Clean House All the Time" philosophy. Unfortunately, I believe I developed a "Clean it When I Notice It" approach to cleansing.

On top of my convoluted method of sanitizing, I am saddled with a persistent compulsion to concoct and make "cool" things. You know — sewing something, knitting a thing, beading a whatsit, crafting a doodad. The creative, fun stuff. All the housework avoidance projects.

Pity my poor husband.

> **"My idea of housework is to sweep the room with a glance."**
> **- Erma Bombeck**

Successful Blending

This is not a cooking column.

At this time in history, blended families are fairly common and an accepted way of life for many family groups. Every one of these blends has a story — some sad, some not, but always interesting.

My remembrance of the first meeting with my ex-husband's new girlfriend was very surprising and definitely memorable. I worked weekends while our two small children, Jenny, five years old and Mike, aged two, stayed with their Dad (my ex-partner). I was popping into the shopping mall to pick up some supplies, on my way home from work. Walking towards me was a pleasant looking woman, whom I had never met, with my two kids in tow!

Emily Post does not have an etiquette solution for this situation. What to do?

The lady, who by this time, realized that I must be the mother of the two munchkins draped around my legs, took the situation in hand and introduced herself. We proceeded to chat for half an hour in the middle of the mall, thus beginning the unusual and convivial relationship we have to this day.

Time passed, and the pleasant woman married our children's father and became a step-mother. To that union she brought her two children, who happened to be a girl and boy the same age as my two kiddos. Built-in playmates!

Some settling-in twinges occurred, but overall the new living arrangements were very satisfactory. I believe these circumstances helped Jenny and Mike to become more resilient and adaptable. They understood that different households had different rules and expectations. Because I worked weekends, Jen and Mike spent Saturdays and Sundays living in their urban home, having a town experience, and had their rural life during the weekdays.

A wide variety of new relationships ensued. Step-grandparents, step-cousins, step-aunts and step-uncles swelled their circle of relations. Even the ex-mother-in-law of their step-mother took my children into her heart. (Boy, these relationship explanations can be confusing!) There are just a few more relations to throw into the mix before I cease with the family tree stuff.

On my family front, I acquired a new husband with whom I bore two more male offspring. The expanded family again had increased!

Back to the important point to this true tale. Being a step-mother can be a very difficult balancing act, especially if you already have two of your own kids to deal with. I know I am very intimidated by the entire concept.

It is long overdue that I thank my children's step-mum, Glenys Soganic, for all the juggling she has done over the years, with and for my two progeny. The driving back and forth, sleepovers with Jen and Mike's friends at her house, the noise, the mess, the confusion!

I would lastly like to thank and acknowledge my ex-husband, Jim Soganic, who, even though we couldn't continue our union, has continued to be a fabulous father and a constant positive influence in our offsprings' lives.

Divorce doesn't always end in an emotional morass. I am saying that, with a lot of cooperation and the keeping of children's welfare in the forefront, blending families can be done.

When Jenny was 13 years old, I asked her if I had ruined her life by divorcing her father. She looked very surprised by my question. She explained she loved her diverse living circumstances and all the special people she had gained as a result.

I love a happy ending, don't you?

Of Attics and Treasures

My grandparents' house didn't have an attic. It had lots of other fascinating attributes, though. An outhouse, a banister to slide down, and the best water, ever, hand-pumped in their porch and drunk out of an old aluminum dipper. Oh yes, and a graveyard right across the street.

I subconsciously missed that non-existent attic, but didn't realize what I was missing until I walked into my first second-hand store at the age of 16. It was a revelation! All those pre-owned clothes, pre-loved toys and well-worn kitchen implements. That was the beginning of a life-long hobby/obsession.

My younger sister, Janine, on the other hand, on this first foray into treasure heaven, looked at the array of goods displayed and pronounced it all JUNK! "What if someone saw us in here?" she whispered. I quickly pointed out to her that the people who would be seeing us would be in the store also.

That was in the days before it became trendy to shop used goods. Recycling wasn't a word that had started to be bandied about yet. Oh, what innocents we were.

At first I shopped mainly for clothes. As time slipped by and my family grew, I found appropriate furniture, toys and sewing fabrics. Most of my choices in these treasure dens were necessities, but I have bought the odd frivolous item. I have fallen in love with a colourful garment that wasn't my size. At the price charity shops charge, I could justify having complete wardrobes in sizes 10, 12 and 14. I did tend to vary sizes, what with pregnancies every few years or so.

Are you wondering about my varied wardrobe being out of date? Well, let me explain my "style". Someone once described my attire as Punk Frump. Enough said.

My favourite purchase, hands down, was an amazing wonderwork. Our six-year-old son, Rudy, had being asking for a guitar. I had been explaining why that wasn't going to happen. More than once I patiently explicated that the purchase of such a musical instrument was out of my financial reach. Then we reached the door of my favourite second-hand retail store.

As we stepped through the doorway, one of the volunteers came from the back sorting room and deposited, right in front of us, a guitar. Not only was it a full-sized guitar, it was a $5.00 guitar. A magical, affordable guitar. It was a Rudy-sized miracle guitar!

I would love to report that he turned out to be a natural instrumentalist, but this is real life and the instrument was tossed aside in short order. But I wouldn't have missed that experience for anything!

If you have never tried a recycled treasure store, go there soon. You might just find your heart's guitar.

(Rudy with prized guitar, 1998)

Acknowledgments

I have been talking about writing and having this book published for SO LONG that I know all my friends, and especially my family, will be very relieved to finally see this book "in the flesh", so to speak! Thanks to all for your patience and not screaming "FINALLY" when I hand your copy to you.

To my lifetime main squeeze, Peter Brown — my eternal thanks for all the chaos you have endured over nearly 40 years.

Gail Nash has earned her weight in the Fudge Fairy's fudge as payment for her astounding editing magic. I have learned so much from her patient editing sessions and am so grateful she volunteered to edit this collection for me.

Thanks to the Writing Group at the Juan de Fuca Seniors Centre for years of encouragement, laughter, and sharing of literary tips and tricks. A five-star nod to our fearless leader, Rick Mickelson, who was instrumental in giving me a final big shove toward my publishing finish line, and steering me to Zoe Duff, of Filidh Publishing.

Zoe saw something in the three sample stories I took to our first meeting, and bravely decided to take a chance on this grey-haired, slightly eccentric, very messy, neophyte writer. An infinite amount of thank-yous for your belief in me, Zoe.

Thanks also to the many people who are named in this book, and all those who inspired me to write: friends, neighbours, family and random strangers.

To my awesome kids, thanks for letting me be your Mom all these years. This book is your legacy from me.

Afterword

I'll bet you are curious as to what I am writing for my second book. It will probably contain another 50 tiny tales. Our defunct SeaShine Smoked Octopus business will be discussed, as well as how to make the right decisions when one "unhoards" the sewing room.

Here are some burning questions that may, or may not, be answered:

1. Will I divulge the Fudge Fairy's recipes?
2. Does chaos still define my life?
3. Did I ever find my green bowl?
4. What is my favourite colour?
5. Do I inadvertently turn my granddaughters into hoarders?

Stay tuned, Earthlings.

Happily,

Charmaine.

About the Author

Charmaine Welch blissfully lives with her main squeeze and the love of her life, Peter Brown, in idyllic Metchosin, which is a rural suburb of Victoria, BC. Their home can be found in various states of disarray, depending on what housework avoidance project Charmaine is working on at the time.